PETER TAYLOR

A Study of the Short Fiction

Twayne's Studies in Short Fiction

Gordon Weaver, General Editor
Oklahoma State University

Peter Taylor, 1986.
Photograph courtesy of J. William Broadway.

PETER TAYLOR

A Study of the Short Fiction

James Curry Robison
Brentwood Academy

TWAYNE PUBLISHERS • _BOSTON_
A Division of G. K. Hall & Co.

Twayne's Studies in Short Fiction Series No. 3
Editorial Assistant to Gordon Weaver: Stephanie Corcoran

Copyediting supervised by Barbara Sutton.
Book design and production by Janet Zietowski.
Typeset in 10/12 Caslon by Compset, Inc.

Printed on permanent/durable acid-free paper
and bound in the United States of America.

Library of Congress Cataloging-in-Publication Data

Robison, James Curry.
 Peter Taylor : a study of the short fiction / James Curry Robison.
  p. cm.—(Twayne's studies in short fiction ; TSSF 3)
 Bibliography: p.
 Includes index.
 ISBN 0-8057-8303-2
 1. Taylor, Peter Hillsman, 1917–   —Criticism and interpretation.
I. Title II. Series.
PS3539.A9633Z87   1988
813'.54—dc19   88-11139
                                                              CIP

To my grandfather
John Curry Vaughan
and my father
David McGill Robison
whose stories taught me to listen.

Contents

Preface

Peter Taylor has published one poem, two novels, two full-length plays, eight one-act plays, and fifty-seven short stories. His reputation has been built on the short stories he produced with striking craft and at a modest rate over fifty years. Since the 1960s critics have typically praised his work in one breath and asked in the next why so fine a writer has been so little known and so little read. As good an answer as any appeared in Albert J. Griffith's *Peter Taylor* in 1970. Professor Griffith concludes, first, that publishing short stories has not built the fame that putting the same amount of effort into writing novels would have and, second, that a subtle style that avoids fads draws little attention. In this first book on Taylor, Griffith provides commentary on all of his published work up to 1969, as well as a useful biography and an exhaustive bibliography. In 1983 a needed bibliographical supplement came from professors Victor A. Kramer—*Andrew Lytle, Walker Percy, Peter Taylor: A Reference Guide.* The thoroughness of professors Griffith and Kramer has been a tremendous asset in my research for this book. Considering how well they assembled the available data in their books, I will not attempt to improve on their bibliographical work, only to build on their formidable contributions. Further, the scope of Griffith's commentary is far broader than mine, my exclusive concern here being Taylor's stories, and not all of them.

Peter Taylor's short fiction is now widely available in three volumes: *The Collected Stories of Peter Taylor* (1969), *In the Miro District and Other Stories* (1977), and *The Old Forest and Other Stories* (1985). Having reprinted several works from collections that are out of print, these books present forty-three of Taylor's pieces; thus most of his stories, particularly his favorites, are available. Of these I will discuss twenty-six representative ones, hoping to provide enough information within a limited scope to assist the reader in drawing conclusions about the remaining pieces. Part 1 of this book is a critical essay on the twenty-six stories mentioned, with introductory and concluding remarks, and five sections in which the works are discussed in a generally chronological order. The writer is the focus of part 2, which contains interviews and

Preface

personal reminiscences, to give the reader a sense of the personality behind the stories. Part 3 contains excerpts from some of the most enlightening essays on Taylor's stories.

My purpose in this book is not to be all-inclusive, as Professor Griffith was in his indispensable study. Rather, my intent is to give the reader a sense of Peter Taylor's place in the world of contemporary short fiction. By looking briefly at the influences on his work, then thoroughly at the features of theme and style that distinguish his stories, I hope to show points of constancy and change that have emerged in Taylor's fiction in the progress of his long career. My emphasis is textual, devoted to assisting the reader in seeing the relationship between theme and technique. Having paid close attention to selected stories, I will then comment on the cumulative effects that they generate and point out some of Taylor's contributions to the genre.

I must thank Peter Taylor for allowing me to quote freely from his works and for granting me the time for several telephone conversations and a personal interview. Mr. Taylor was always responsive, informative, and gracious.

For their vital help in assembling the manuscript of this book, I am indebted to Mary Ellen Price and Janet Greenfield—former students, occasional typists, enduring friends. Thanks also to Ron Medlin for his proofreading and comments.

James Curry Robison

Brentwood Academy

Part 1

THE SHORT FICTION:
A CRITICAL ANALYSIS

Introduction

Reputation

Between the time I committed myself to writing this book in February 1986 and the time I actually started to write in the summer, the reputation of Peter Taylor changed substantially. Granted, his work has been read for years by fiction writers, serious students of the short story, students of Southern literature, and subscribers to the *New Yorker* and the *Sewanee Review*. But all of those readers put together would not add a percentage point on a Gallup poll. Being known and admired by literature teachers and subscribers to elite magazines may be comforting, even vindicating, but such an audience is too small to get the writer's name into the casual conversation of the general reader. What does get people talking about writers is that raw American stimulus, publicity.

Within six months in 1986, Peter Taylor got more publicity than he had received altogether in his previous fifty years of writing. In May of 1986 he received the PEN/Faulkner Award for the best volume of fiction in 1985 for *The Old Forest and Other Stories*. The award got his name, and often his picture, into mass-market magazines, which had reviewed his earlier collections but generated no enthusiasm. The subtext of these generally positive reviews was: This man is a good writer who really deserves to be read, but, dear reader, we realize that you will never find the time. At least we have met our responsibility and told you about his new book. With the coverage of his PEN/Faulkner Award, Taylor's name became one of those conversational signs, a name that could be used only by those who got all the way back to the book review sections of *Time* and *Newsweek*. Knowing who he was, not to mention having bought a copy of *The Old Forest*, was cocktail-party proof that the person giving testimony was well read and, possibly, a deep thinker.

Then in September 1986 *A Summons to Memphis* appeared, a full-scale novel from the short story writer whose only other "novel" was really a novella (*A Woman of Means*, 1950). Put in crude terms, the book

3

was a hit. Then came more bold-print coverage, more positive reviews, more mass-media enthusiasm, than the previous book attracted. By Christmas of 1986, anyone who fancied himself a reader had to know who Peter Taylor was and should have bought at least one of his two new releases. As if the whole literary world were determined to compensate Taylor for years of ignored craftsmanship, April 1987 was the harvest month. On the sixth he received the $50,000 annual Ritz Hemingway literary prize, and on the sixteenth he received the Pulitzer Prize—both for *A Summons to Memphis.*

This late and decisive rise in an author's fame poses a natural question: What took him so long? The strange answer: Nothing. Peter Taylor has been writing essentially the same kind of fiction since 1937. He has refined his work, gone through some impressive experiments, written several plays, but "The Fancy Woman," published in the *Southern Review* at Louisiana State University in 1941, will not suffer from comparison with the best stories the *New Yorker* published this year. The proper question is: What took American readers so long?

Two things: first, there is nothing topical or trendy in a Peter Taylor story; second, he writes subdued stories. When he started publishing before World War II, the fashions of the era were the chill existentialism of Hemingway, the naturalism of Farrell and Steinbeck, the glossy urban realism of O'Hara and Cheever. The point is not that there was anything wrong with these varieties of fiction. The point is that they were not *Taylor's* variety. His stories did not even fit the bill entirely for an editor who wanted "Southern" fiction. Taylor's stories were not as baroque as Faulkner's or as funny and grotesque as Erskine Caldwell's. Then came the social changes of the sixties and seventies, and American life reflected a new outlook in clothes, hairstyles, politics, music, and not least—in fiction. "Innovative fiction" appeared, "nonfiction" novels and "antistory" stories. The stories most popular with critics presented indecipherable narrative sequences, multiple realities, incoherent narrators, surrealism, and incongruous combinations of action, subjects, and language. In 1969, when experimentalism was nearing high tide, Peter Taylor published "Dean of Men," a beautifully crafted, subdued, and ironic story. It is full of conflict and emotional complexity, without a trace of experimentalism. A Taylor story read along with other stories from that era sounds like a Stradivarius in the midst of electric guitars.

A look at the *New York Times Book Review* of 19 October 1969 will illustrate the literary climate that turned him into an anomaly. On opposing pages in this issue are reviews of Robert Coover's *Pricksongs and Descants* and Taylor's *Collected Stories*.[1] Coover, typical of the experimental writers who dominated American fiction from 1965 to 1975, was not satisfied with literature as a sequence of words. As the review by philosopher and fellow experimental writer William H. Gass states, Coover wanted more—he wanted the effect of a fugue. One of the best-known stories in the book is "The Babysitter," in which he creates a broken, reiterated narrative by retelling parts of the story in varying versions until what really happens is anybody's guess. His technique is cinematic: intercutting scenes, maintaining the frenetic movement of jump cuts, finally generating a montage of images, phrases, and possibilities. His purpose in offering several versions of what happens to the babysitter is to emphasize doubt, confusion, and anxiety.

Taylor, however, has always been satisfied to show moral turmoil and anxiety without trying to inflict them on his reader. A perfect example of his approach is "Dean of Men," first anthologized in *Collected Stories*, and perfectly typical in subject matter and style. Like Coover, he shows a tormented man; but instead of bombarding the reader with a blur of images, he calmly undercuts his misguided narrator with revealing incidents. His fiction does not read like a movie script; it reads like a story. Reviewer Richard Howard commented: "Affable, persuasive, never glossy, never hurrying, steadily gaining ground, these narratives are not glamorous or side-splitting or desperate."[2] In the sixties, defiance for its own sake was often considered an adequate cause for attacking established institutions and social forms.

Though Peter Taylor did not reflect the spirit of the age in his work, he has never defended narrowness or reactionary thinking. He seems to have been as much amused as influenced by the Southern Agrarians. Often he challenges complacency and tries to jar his reader; nevertheless, his writing has always been that of a gentleman. As everyone raised in the South knows, even after the tidal wave of the sixties washed over the land and receded, a gentleman does not disturb or insult people to amuse himself. Joyce Carol Oates observed, "Taylor's writing is always impeccable: he is a gentleman confiding in another gentleman"[3] when he addresses his reader. In the wake of the Free Speech Movement and Abbie Hoffman's radical disruption of language and mores, the demand for gentlemen in the cultural life of the nation was at its lowest ebb in 1969. In the mood of the age, in an essay that appeared in the *Hudson Review* in early 1970, Roger Sale deemed Ronald Sukenick's *The Death of the Novel and Other Stories* a fine achievement, while complaining that Taylor's collection was merely "precious."[4] If responses like this are sufficiently widespread among readers, even if not among literary professionals, a writer's reputation will not grow.

The few hostile critiques of Taylor's short fiction may, like Sale's, say what many readers have thought. In a 1969 review Barbara Raskin stated that the new collection "is respectable, careful, craftsman-like, but ultimately mind-deadening."[5] She added that the "Jamesian precision" and "Faulknerian mood" are wasted on "sympathetic accounts of white women whining" and the fact that Miss Lenoras still exist is not sufficient reason to write about them: "We've had enough old-style, southern-fried realism." In the following month Jonathan Yardley wrote a vigorous rejoinder to Raskin's "savage and self-indulgent" review.[6] He made a case against her "Dixiephobia" and for Taylor's characters having the same value as those of Bernard Malamud and Robert Coover. Yardley's defense is convincing, but since enough people think as Raskin does—and apparently they have for decades—then the indifference of the masses has overcome the enthusiasm of most critics where Taylor is concerned.

The final complaint against Taylor's fiction I will address may reveal the greatest single obstacle to his fame: his subtle narrative technique. In a 1977 issue of the *New York Times Book Review*, Anatole Broyard noted that "In the Miro District"

> moves like a heavily-loaded wagon. [Taylor] would as soon sit on his hat as compress his effects. He writes as if he came from a place where no one ever interrupts while you are talking, where civility is prized above all else and ceremony scrupulously observed. One can imagine "The Captain's Son" and "In the Miro District" being narrated from a rocker or a chair on a porch. The author is in no hurry to develop his theme, and there is in his manner a complacent, and sometimes irritating, assumption that you are willing to hear him out.
>
> Mr. Taylor seems not to have noticed that the age has accelerated its grimacing, that current fiction has seen fit to complicate itself.[7]

Here, observations that appear to be intended as criticism turn out to be simple statements of fact, none of which show faults. To say that Taylor's stories develop too slowly is like complaining that Mozart used too many notes, that Monet painted fuzzy images, that Marcel Marceau does not speak up. Tone is the distinguishing feature of a Taylor story, and in order for point of view and diction to evoke, then modulate, the tone, the writer must have time. Yes, these stories do develop slowly, but the sound of the teller's voice, his vocabulary, syntax, rhythms, a sense of his personality—all take time to establish. The style of his writing is necessarily unhurried. And of course Taylor does come from a place where well-bred people do not interrupt and civility is important. He was born in the South and has spent most of his life there. Since he no doubt heard many stories that he would use delivered to the rhythm of a porch rocker, he often passes on that rhythm undisturbed.

Not wanting to offend a reader, he would surely tell someone who finds his stories too slow to put them down, by all means. He is also certainly aware of how fiction has "seen fit to complicate itself" in the last twenty years, but perhaps he would argue that fiction lacks the individual volition to become complicated without the help of writers. He has not chosen to be such a writer. In short, Anatole Broyard's grievances are based on differences of opinion and taste, not on aesthetic or technical flaws in Taylor's work.

These stories are not for everybody, but they inspire great enthusiasm in readers who find Taylor capable of rare subtlety and a light touch. Keith Opdahl seems to be a much more patient reader than Broyard: "Imagine what Hemingway lacks in his stories, and you will have imagined Mr. Taylor's strength. The groping, the reserve, the infinite need, the endless guessing of another's mind—they're all here. . . . These stories are the kind that one cites to define a certain quality of life."[8] John Thompson was able to compress his evaluation of Taylor's effect into one word: "Peter Taylor may have been denied his place on the big electric scoreboard not only because of his modesty but also because he has in very large supply that quality that leads almost as certainly to underestimation as earnest pompousness does to overestimation, and that is, charm. His stories are beguiling, humorous, enfolding; no matter how grim their judgment you feel better reading them than you do when you are doing most other things, you want to go on: charm."[9] Peter Taylor has been the victim of his virtues.

Influences

Since the 1950s Taylor's reputation as a writer's writer and his self-confidence have been sustained by the praise of a small but prestigious readership. He has been nourished by the enthusiasm of readers like Robert Lowell, Randall Jarrell, Allen Tate, and Robert Penn Warren until finally the "master of the short-story form" has been acknowledged by the rank and file of book reviewers. Having sat in the classes of Tate and John Crowe Ransom, and having roomed with Robert Lowell and lived in the same house with Randall Jarrell before he was halfway through college, Taylor began his career as a writer in such distinguished company that just meeting the norm of that group set him well above the mass of fiction writers, new and old. He also brought with him considerable insight and experience with literature. Allen Tate commented, "I was Peter's first college English teacher, but I found I could not teach him anything, so I asked him to leave the class after about two weeks."[10]

He came to college knowing more about literature than most English majors ever learn, and at Vanderbilt and then at Kenyon, he found himself in the midst of a group of energetic poet/critics, an odd place for a storyteller, but a stimulating one. He wrote some poems to please "Mr. Ransom" and pleased him well enough to get the only poem he has published into the *Kenyon Review* in 1939.[11] He also married a poet, Eleanor Ross. He has always been encompassed before and behind by poets, but many of them have also written fiction: his wife, short stories; Jarrell, *Pictures from an Institution;* Tate, *The Fathers;* and most notably, Warren, *All the King's Men,* an extraordinary popular and critical success known for the poetic rhythms of Jack Burden's narrating voice.

Meanwhile, at a painstaking pace Taylor continued to produce stories, rehearsing the first sentences for several days, getting the sound, the rhythm, the tone—just as a poet does before going to the next line. He has mentioned in interviews that he does not outline stories or try to force them when the words will not come. Rather he writes the first few paragraphs, having an idea where he is going, and listens for the right words as he proceeds, like a poet. Poetic rhythm and vigor, shaped into a story with conversational looseness, is a hallmark of Taylor's style.

That conversational looseness, that charming, relaxed narrative from a rocking chair that the reader can hear in Taylor's stories, comes from his childhood. In the long tradition of Southern storytellers, his apprenticeship as a fiction writer began with the stories he heard in Tennessee as a child. Both of his grandfathers were politicians (one served three terms as governor and was a famous raconteur), and his great-uncle was also a governor and lived until Taylor was fourteen, passing on the stories and style of the Old South. The dedication of *Collected Stories* reads:

> For my Mother
> Katherine Taylor Taylor
> who was the best teller of tales I know
> and from whose lips I first heard many
> of the stories in this book.[12]

Peter Taylor, though his work is known for its elegance and polish, is a natural storyteller. His family background, his social milieu, and his academic experience all seasoned his innate gifts.

Beyond the fertile influence of friends and family, Taylor has also felt the impact of a force that shaped all of them (except Lowell)—growing up in the South. His stories are usually set in Tennessee, and in large measure they display traits typical of Southern literature: a sense of place, the influence of history, a reverence for language, and a holistic worldview. Places, especially the distinctions between places, are important in his fiction, whether he is making the distinction between the country and the city or between one city and another. His favorite contrast is between Nashville and Memphis, which would be presumed quite alike by those who do not know them. History is not so powerful in Taylor's work as in Warren's and Faulkner's, where the past often overwhelms the present, but it is still a shaping force. The history of the South, of the county, of the family, is never far from the thoughts of his characters, and it conveys to them the sins of their fathers along with a vision of genteel and purposeful lives. As for the holistic worldview, the Southerner is traditionally less concerned with analytical thinking and more concerned with synthesizing experience, seeing relationships between things, drawing useful conclusions.

As Taylor's handling of locale and character shows his meticulous eye for detail, so does his diction exhibit to a high degree his sensitive ear and his reverence for the spoken word. In his pages the dialogue of whites, high- and low-class, and of blacks, respectable and not, is completely accurate. Even more, his narrative voice establishes the melodic line that sustains his stories. Sometimes it comes straight from a first-person narrative persona, and sometimes it is a third-person rendition of a character's thoughts amplified. I will devote considerable attention to voice later, noting that his concern with the sound of the spoken word issues from a powerful Southern tradition is enough for now.

Finally there are two other Southern traits that appear only faintly in his stories: the grotesque and the influence of Christianity. For perspective on both, I call on the essays of Flannery O'Connor collected in *Mystery and Manners*. Defending her own use of the grotesque, she stated (of a public not generally attuned to her values), "To the hard of hearing you shout, and for the almost-blind you draw large and startling figures."[13] Taylor may agree that the reading public ignores important matters, but he rarely resorts to shock. He uses grotesque characters and incidents sparingly, preferring to lead his reader gently, or in Emily Dickinson's words, to "dazzle gradually." Of course he does use grotesque characters effectively in stories such as "A Spinster's Tale," "Venus, Cupid, Folly and Time," "A Friend and Protector," and "The Hand of Emmagene." These stories prove his skill in the subgenre, but the small number of them indicates that he prefers a subtler method. As for Christianity, it is certainly part of the background, but it never bears heavily on his characters or on their decisions. Its importance is no more than that of an accurate detail on a stage backdrop. For O'Connor the South is not "Christ-centered," but it is "Christ-haunted."[14] Taylor's upper-class urban folk, however, do not feel haunted at all.

Though the influences of colleagues, family, and region account for much of what is striking about Taylor's work, the writers he has studied also echo in his passages. He has frequently taught himself, and the students in his writing classes, by reading the masters of fiction. He has been compared most often to Anton Chekhov and Henry James, less frequently to Ivan Turgenev, Leo Tolstoy, Jane Austen, W. M. Thackeray, James Joyce, and Frank O'Connor. He has mentioned his admiration of all these, as well as Marcel Proust, Anthony Trollope, D. H. Lawrence, Thomas Mann, and William Faulkner. Judging from his comments, he rereads these writers first for pleasure, then to feel the total effect of their narratives. Only after reading many times does he focus on specific points of technique. Looking in one glance at all the ideas and styles these authors present can be confusing; however, they can be loosely grouped.

Generally speaking, these writers tend to be Victorians or realists. Victorian values and style appear in Austen (I am stretching the literary period here), Thackeray, and Trollope, and realistic details abound in Russians Turgenev, Tolstoy, and Chekhov, Frenchman Proust, American James, Englishman Lawrence, German Mann, and Irishman O'Connor. Though realism is not an adequate heading for Joyce and Faulkner, they wrote their early work in that vein before growing beyond it. In broad terms the Victorians and the realists mentioned here, all concerned with fiction of manners, as Taylor is, have exerted a collective influence on his work. Perhaps the most identifiable influence is that of Henry James, an American realist whose Anglophilia (which Taylor shares) makes him a composite Victorian-realist. Considering the similar concern with decorum shared by Victorians and their Southern coevals, there seems to be more truth than error in thinking of Taylor's style as that of a Victorian-realist.

Uniqueness

The fact that so many writers have influenced Taylor raises a question: How many writers can he resemble before the influences become so multiple and blended that Taylor is simply unique? These influences blend, flow into the deeper currents from his friends and family, and finally join the rising mainstream of his original gifts. The result is a fully realized artist: a writer whose work, rooted in his rich origins and nourished by broad reading, is patrician without haughtiness, meticulous without tediousness, sophisticated without condescension.

In his unobtrusive blend of subject matter and technique, Peter Taylor has effectively set himself apart from other fiction writers. Nothing he does is eye-catching; rather the very moderation and constancy in his stories have persisted until he is not quite like any of those great writers who influenced his development and not at all like any of his contemporaries. He is a Victorian-realist from the urban South, one who is not altogether pleased with the twentieth-century world but has made his peace with it. Despite the engaging reminiscent tone of his narratives, he is not longing for the past but merely savoring it, using it to enrich and stabilize his modern world.

He often presents sympathetic characters who enjoy city life, parties, and the comforts of money, just as he does. Robert Penn Warren was the first to notice Taylor's subgenre in 1948: "Peter Taylor's stories are officially about the contemporary, urban, middle-class world of the upper South, and he is the only writer who has taken this as his province. . . . It is a world . . . caught in a tangle of modern commercialism and traditions and conventions gone to seed, confused among pieties and pretensions."[15] Though the collapse of the old Southern order, and the attendant damage to the family, concern Taylor, "he regards the process without too much distress." He is not an elegist of the Old South but an ironic commentator on the modern South. Warren has said that Taylor has "a disenchanted mind, but a mind that nevertheless understands and values enchantment."[16]

Although Taylor's world is sometimes called middle- and upper-middle class, it seems to me more often upper class. There are certainly stories of servants and academics and others who are outside the aristocracy; but by conventional standards, wealthy people who spend their weekends at the country club and their summers in the mountains have effectively sealed themselves into the upper class.

In his typical settings Taylor shows characters who variously observe or abuse decorum and face the consequences. Depending on the individuals and their problems, decorum may be a mantle or a yoke, but the weight (of family tradition, obligation, and social inertia) always falls on his characters. These people deal with powerful expectations, with manners, with crucial things unsaid. Frequently in his scenes, the unspoken words are the most important ones. Beneath whatever harmony exists, there is also discord in his stories, and his principal characters always have to face some sort of alienation—from the past, from family, or from peers.

Ironically, decorum, intended as a means to gracious living, often causes alienation; but it sometimes limits the damage done by alienation by preventing a wounded character from cutting himself off utterly from others, because that would be a breach of good manners. In this narrow world, Taylor's stories are still vivid enough to have thematic significance beyond the country club, the columned house, and the mountain cottage. T. D. Young has stated, "What he presents is something that is always significant, usually much broader in application than the precisely delineated world in which it occurs, and nearly always unsettling or disturbing."[17]

Because of the restraint with which Taylor's narrators tell their tales, their attitude is sometimes ambiguous. Many critics mention the humor of the narrators and the warmth of their stories. Stephen Goodwin said of *Collected Stories*, "Our consolation is in the tone of his prose; [his] stories are so full of warmth, of concern and insight, that we must take heart."[18] Also referring to *Collected Stories*, William Peden stated a few months later, "His vision is extremely austere. . . . The author usually views his people from afar, as it were; there is little warmth in his work."[19] Perhaps the mild but ironic tone of these stories inclines critics to react differently. The greater the room for interpretation, the likelier the reader is to find whatever he seeks.

Irony and subtlety are Taylor's typical means of presenting his themes; further, he has commented over the years that he is more concerned with presenting his characters than with constructing plots or making statements of theme. Again like many realists (like Chekhov, who gives revealing glimpses of people's lives, or like James, whose architectonic plots hold a central intelligence), Taylor devotes most of his attention to character. In his late period, however, he has paid more attention to plot, as evidenced by stories in *In the Miro District and Other Stories* and by the two new tales in *The Old Forest and Other Stories*. In William Peden's words, "The drama of Peter Taylor's stories tends to be internal. It exists in and flows from the inner lives of his people. . . . Character, indeed, *is* the story."[20] The tales are frequently "told by a narrator who is urbane, witty, sophisticated, nostalgic—very much like Taylor himself—a gentleman who is confiding in a lady or another gentleman."[21] As Walter Clemons has noted, "He simply buttonholes you and starts telling you things. When he's done, he's anatomized a society. His stories have the resonance of novels."[22]

And even though this well-bred speaker is restrained, a turbulent undercurrent runs beneath the narrative surface, what Richard Eder has labeled "a loss of patrician assurance."[23] As decorum has inherent virtues and vices, so does the restraint that it encourages. Restraint may prevent unpleasant scenes between people whose ideas clash, but it may also prevent cleansing honesty. One of the negative by-products of restraint is that it deepens the alienation of characters who already lack openness. "Patrician assurance" has sustained aristocrats through loneliness and frustration; a gentleman who has done the right thing in a difficult situation can comfort himself in the belief that his behavior will be vindicated ultimately. When this assurance crumbles, so do the old patterns of behavior.

Whether the reader finds the tone comic or tragic, warm or austere, Taylor relies on a distinctive voice to carry his stories, to engage the reader: "Like Lawrence's, Taylor's stories rely to a great extent on their rhythm. That is, the story's life (the life of its people) is deeply dependent on the way it is told."[24] Combined with recurrent themes of decorum and alienation is Taylor's tone. I am using tone to mean the linguistic and dramatic atmosphere a story evokes. It is the product of numerous contributing factors often known collectively as style. To an obvious degree, subject matter, setting, and characters lay the foundation for style in a story; but point of view, diction, syntax, and narrative sequence are the bricks and mortar of style. Two of Taylor's later stories provide good examples: "In the Miro District" (1977) and "The Old Forest" (1979). Both of these are told by first-person narrators as recollections from many years before. They tell of initiation experiences from young manhood: in the first, the eighteen-year-old boy has three decisive "face-offs" with his grandfather; in the second, Nat Ramsey is almost rejected by Caroline, who is now, as he tells the story, his wife of forty years. Both stories deal with life-shaping incidents, but the narrators are far enough removed in time that their points of view are ironic and somewhat detached.

Of course the diction of "The Fancy Woman" and "Bad Dreams" reflects the lower-class origins of the viewpoint characters, but more often the characters are members of the Southern aristocracy and the narrator's language echoes theirs. In a revealing segment of his essay "The Nashville Stories," Herschel Gower noted, "One contribution to the texture [of Taylor's stories] is the diction, which is faintly old-fashioned if not outright archaic."[25] He proceeded to list the preferences of the Nashville upper class: "boarding school" not "prep school," "toddies" not "cocktails," "sitting room" not "living room," resort "cottages" not "cabins," "quarrel" not "fight," and "people of means" not the "very rich." In the upper-class South, one of the strongest features of decorum is that it dictates adherence to proper language, an adherence rarely discussed but vigorously observed. Another way of looking at the diction in Taylor's stories is to acknowledge that considerable vocabulary and word combinations are automatically unavailable to his well-bred narrators. Like Taylor, they know a great deal that they would never dream of saying, and in narrating from their elegant and restricted lexicon, Taylor puts the reader deeply into their world in a matter of a few paragraphs.

Weaving point of view and diction together, Taylor uses a syntax and narrative sequence peculiar to his fiction. Albert J. Griffith stated that "his favorite method is the digressive-progressive memoir story, which leisurely builds characterizations and releases the meaning in a story without any great show of effects."[26] Neither "In the Miro District" nor "The Old Forest" is in any hurry. The narrators move back and forth in time as impulse and logical associations cause them to. This method of revelation makes the stories wider, meandering, circling around the focal action and enriching it by background, comment, and diction. The stories of the late period take this technique to the greatest extreme, becoming as deep and wide as they are long. His style is built on backing up and filling in, on elaborating like the storytellers he grew up listening to. Whereas Chekhov wanted to tell the middle of a story and delete the rest, Taylor is quite concerned with the rest, with illuminating concentric layers of meaning that mount up beyond the central action. Only after the reader has absorbed the environment and voice of the story is he prepared to grasp its meaning. Like Tolstoy, Taylor wants to saturate the reader in the milieu of each story. Thus before he resolves the problems of grandson and grandfather or of Nat and Caroline, he immerses us in their worlds.

In a review of *The Old Forest and Other Stories* Robert Towers commented on this technique: "The fact that Peter Taylor's stories are like miniature novels has been noted before. His narrative method is to hover over the action, to digress from it, to explore the byways and relationships, to speculate on alternative possibilities—in short to defy the conventions of brevity and concentration that we usually associate with the genre."[27] Like the Victorian and realist novelists he has often read, he wants an expansive richness—a complete feel for the characters' world and the narrator's language. Like the vigorous lyric poets under whom he studied, he wants decisive impact and poetic resonance. Resembling the falcon of Yeats's "The Second Coming," Taylor's stories move in a "widening gyre," becoming broader as they rise. But unlike Yeats's falcon, Taylor's stories can always "hear the falconer," and the central narrative does not fall apart. The digressions contribute substantially to the tone and substance of the tale.

In the fiction of Peter Taylor can be seen the narrative ease and charm of his mother's stories, the incisiveness of Chekhov, the nuance of James, the grand sweep of Tolstoy. All these sources come together in the city of Taylor's upper South where he builds his own house of fiction. He presents the themes of decorum and alienation and through the techniques of the well-bred point of view, the diction of upper-class Tennessee, and the digressive-progressive narrative.

Overview

Even though Taylor's stories have become somewhat more elaborate over the years, the most striking quality about his work is the similarity in it from 1938 to 1985. Professor Griffith noted in 1970: "Between

Taylor's earliest stories and his latest, then, there has not been any great disparity in subject matter or in theme. Nor has there been any revolutionary shift in artistic method; structure, mood, tone, style, point of view have all developed new potentialities without changing their basic patterns. As early as 'The Scoutmaster' and 'A Long Fourth,' Peter Taylor had already found an appropriate form for his individual vision."[28] This evaluation is still valid regarding the fiction of a man who had set himself a hard task by his twenty-first birthday. Before he had become a legal adult, he had become a mature writer, a fact that escaped neither Allen Tate nor Robert Penn Warren. His early stories were not as consistently strong as later ones, but in one story after another he displayed the steady control of an older writer. He did not yield to temptations to force a plot, unleash grand purple passages, or allow himself the excess of satire where muted irony made a better story.

Of course literary critics are most excited by change in a writer. Whether the change be good or bad, it always provides reason for analysis and comment. Thus even though the critical consensus has heavily favored Taylor's stories, there are to this date relatively few theses and dissertations on his work, a dearth that will doubtless be removed by the recent rise in his fame. In 1961, when critics were occasionally "discovering" Taylor, Walter Sullivan stated that Taylor is "a perceptive artist, a skilled craftsman, and he is the only American in his generation whose work can stand comparison with that of Frank O'Connor and Chekhov and Joyce. From the beginning, Taylor's stories have been original in concept. He was among the first to discover that the Southern city—not town—had literary possibilities."[29] After eleven years, Sullivan's praise faded; he wrote in 1972, "Peter Taylor, skillful as he is, no longer shows us much that is new."[30] Largely true, but hardly a condemnation. When stories from his first years of writing, stories like "A Spinster's Tale," "The Fancy Woman," and "A Long Fourth," can still shame most of what is printed in current issues of the *New Yorker,* what more can one ask of a writer? If he could stand comparison with Chekhov and Joyce in 1961, does he have to do better for an encore in 1972?

After a writer reaches a certain degree of richness and polish, further comparisons and superlatives serve no purpose. But in fairness, the reader of Taylor's work will note that he has done some different things, as shown by the monologue of "The Walled Garden," by the present-tense narration of "Allegiance" and "The Gift of the Prodigal," by the grotesque in "Venus, Cupid, Folly and Time" and "The Hand of Emmagene," and by the verse form in four stories from *In the Miro District*. Taylor has not lacked vitality or a healthy sense of adventure, but he has displayed the good sense to keep writing about what interests him most. The result has been persistent similarities of character and situation between early and late stories. "The Other Times" and "The Old Forest" both deal with the problems upper-class people face when they dabble in adventures beneath their social station. "A Long Fourth" and "The Captain's Son" both show families so afraid of genuine human involvement that they exploit decorum to hide from others. "The Scoutmaster" and "In the Miro District" both present scenes in which the older generation cannot accept the sexual mores of the young. The later stories display the greater sophistication that the reader would expect decades to produce, but the same revealing details, decisive points of conflict, and ironies exist in all of the stories mentioned.

With his *Collected Stories* in 1969 and *The Old Forest and Other Stories* in 1985, Peter Taylor has given his readers a broad selection of his work from the forties, fifties, and sixties. The 1969 volume presents stories from all three decades, while the later contains two new stories but takes all of the rest from the forties and fifties. *The Old Forest* offers four stories each from *A Long Fourth and Other Stories*, *The Widows of Thornton*, and *Happy Families Are All Alike*. Although these 1969 and 1985 volumes largely consist of stories that had already been published in hardcover collections, in 1977 Taylor produced *In the Miro District and Other Stories*, a completely new collection of stories from periodicals of the sixties and seventies. Finally, *The Old Forest* also offers one new piece from 1979 (the title story) and one from 1981 ("The Gift of the Prodigal").

With *Collected Stories* (twenty-one stories), *In the Miro District* (eight), and *The Old Forest* (fourteen), Peter Taylor now has the majority of his stories available to the public (forty-three of fifty-seven published stories). Because these volumes are the ones most accessible to the general reader and because they contain the highlights of Taylor's fifty-year career in publishing short fiction, I will use them as my primary sources.

For convenience I have grouped his stories into early, middle, and late periods based on their dates of first publication. The early group consists of stories published up until 1948, when the first collection, *A Long Fourth and Other Stories*, appeared. The middle stories appeared between 1949 and 1968, and the collections for those years were *The Widows of Thornton* (1954), *Happy Families Are All Alike: A Collection of Stories* (1959), *Miss Lenora When Last Seen and Fifteen Other Stories* (1963), and *The Collected Stories of Peter Taylor* (1969). The only story in the last volume that originally appeared in 1969 was "Dean of Men," which I consider the initial story in Taylor's late period because in length and scope it resembles his other major stories from the 1970s— "The Captain's Son," "In the Miro District," and "The Old Forest." These stories show the artist at the top of his form, and each one deals with relationships so complicated by time, family involvement, or social class that it offers the complexity and resonance of a novel. Additional stories to be discussed in the segment on the late period are "The Hand of Emmagene," "Three Heroines," "The Instruction of a Mistress," "Her Need," "Daphne's Lover," and "The Gift of the Prodigal."

The Early Period

"Human kind cannot bear very much reality," says T. S. Eliot in "Burnt Norton," and his statement could serve well as an epigraph to *A Long Fourth and Other Stories* (1948), especially the four stories considered here. "A Spinster's Tale" and "The Fancy Woman" both have main characters who cannot bear what they find in the world; thus they develop defense systems as means of escaping from the fundamental truths of sex, death, and their social positions. Neither the spinster nor the fancy woman can achieve a healthy balance of sexual expression and decorum. Faced with unpleasant truths, they fly to extremes. Similarly, "The Scoutmaster" and "A Long Fourth" present characters who balk at reality. Facing death and disappointment has caused Uncle Jake, a scoutmaster, to take refuge in childish simplicity, uniforms, and recited ideals. Harriet Wilson, by contrast, has lived by decorum all her life, shielding herself from all unpleasantness by playing her role without question, thought, or depth. The pathetic result is that she has created a household so superficial that neither she nor her children are capable of love. By the time the numbness of the Wilson family becomes apparent, the damage is too great for her to reverse or even to express. In each of these stories, characters who cannot face reality variously abuse decorum as they try to escape the pain of thinking and feeling in difficult situations.

"A Spinster's Tale" (1940)

"A Spinster's Tale,"[31] published in the fall of 1940 in the *Southern Review*, is a story that Peter Taylor finished while he was an undergraduate at Kenyon College. Robert Penn Warren, who accepted the story and two others published in 1941, had earlier rejected two stories that were published in 1937 by *River*, a small Mississippi literary journal. Even though "A Spinster's Tale" was not his first publication, it was the first story of lasting value that Taylor got into print. The story has many qualities typical of those that have followed it. Betsy, the first-person reflective adult narrator, recalls childhood experiences from her thirteenth and fourteenth years, telling a story of a problem—alcoholism—that is both internal and external to her family. Internally, she witnesses her high school brother's regular drinking bouts, while externally, she must watch the drunken, red-faced Mr. Speed staggering past her window several afternoons each week. The setting is Nashville, Church Street to be specific, a street that is downtown-residential when the story takes place. Since her father mentions the "possibilities of a general war" (144), the time is apparently around 1914, when World War I has started in Europe, but the United States has not yet entered. All of these features—the tone, family setting, place, time—are typical, even prophetic, of things to come. Taylor raised an additional point of interest in a 1973 interview.

> There was a period when I tried to see if I could make every speech in the dialogue in a story one that I had heard somewhere. . . . And "A Spinster's Tale" is right out of my mother's mouth. My mother was rather prim and puritanical . . . and that story is really hers. Her mother died when she was fourteen . . . and there was a real Mr. Speed. The language in the story was my mother's too—it's more Victorian, more elevated than the language in most of my stories.[32]

Perhaps the language is more elevated than in his other stories, but the narrator of "A Spinster's Tale" bears a clear resemblance to many narrators from the author's next fifty years of fiction. Like most successful stories, this one also has a powerful opening sentence that sets the tone and hints at the conflict that develops: "My brother would often get drunk when I was a little girl, but that put a different sort of fear into me from what Mr. Speed did" (141).

But having seen how this story fits the pattern of Taylor's later fiction, the reader will notice several departures from the norm. Like his other early stories, this one is highly unified, a quality that loosens in stories from the 1950s and afterward. Similarly, sexual matters are much more pronounced in the early period, whereas later they are subdued or subliminal. Also Mr. Speed is a more grotesque and sensational character than Taylor customarily employs. His drunken stumbling, swearing, and flailing with his cane make him too bizarre not to be shocking, especially to the sheltered narrator. Mr. Speed ultimately raises the fearful mysteries of sex and death: sex, because his violent masculinity, his resemblance to other men and wild horses, suggest the whole world of masculinity, barely restrained violence, and sexuality that Betsy fears; death, because Betsy's world after the death of her mother from childbirth lacks feminine comfort and the soothing reassurance of life as a child wants it. By dying soon after her stillborn infant, Betsy's mother embodies the inexorable blend of sex and death—neither of which Betsy wants to face. Rather, when she is first frightened by *Mr.* Speed (her euphemism to try to make "Old Speed" less crude and threatening), she feels the "sudden inexplicable memory of my mother's cheek and a vision of her in her bedroom on a spring day" (143). Sex and death, natural shocks of adult life, have deprived the pubescent narrator of her mother and of her childhood.

As Betsy fights to preserve her naive state, Taylor's standard technique and themes appear. Imagery establishes a vivid physical world: her brother "putting his white forefinger all over his flushed face and finally over his lips to say, 'Sh-sh-sh-sh!'" (141); Betsy's longing recollection, "my mother's cheek was warm on mine" (144); Speed with "his face, heavy, red, fierce [walking with a] "stomping sort of stagger . . . poking his walnut cane into the soft sod along the sidewalk" (147). As is often the case with Taylor's imagery, in this story it operates at a deeper level than the narrator grasps. She, who now tells the story as a spinster, has clearly rejected sexual involvement and has no idea of all the sexual implications of Mr. Speed's phallic cane; "the three horses running away . . . with little girls riding them" (145); her own "longing for my brother to strike me when he was leaning over me" (151); and her dream of men coming to look at a girl's "giant hands" and shake them "but the little girl was ashamed of them and hid them under her skirt" (155).

The frightened but somewhat detached tone of the story comes from the mixed point of view and from the diction. The tension of the narrative grows from the point of view of the fourteen-year-old child, but the girl's first-person account is filtered through the spinster's reflection, making the experiences less shocking. The diction, as well, moderates her fear and the tempestuous close of the story. With Speed having fallen from the porch where he has shouted at Betsy and her maid, Betsy's fear of harm has passed. Now as she waits for the Black Maria (the police van) to take Mr. Speed to jail, she says, "I found I was capable of . . . cruelty [and] was afraid to go minister to the helpless old Mr. Speed" (166). The combination of narrative distance over time and restrained language enables Taylor to tell the story vividly

21

while maintaining complete control. This story about fear and frenzy never becomes frenzied itself.

From these well-managed narrative techniques come thematic concerns that have continued to appear in Taylor's fiction. Despite the noted peculiarities of this story's surface action, typical themes still move beneath the surface and finally emerge: decorum, betrayal, alienation, and the passage of time. One reason that Mr. Speed is such a threat is that this pathetic, drunken creature is beyond respect for himself or others. Beyond the bounds of common decency, he lives drunk, disheveled, swearing, oblivious to others, and useless to himself. He observes no conventional rules of behavior, which are the traditional restraints on masculine conduct, violence, and sexual aggression—all merging into one in Betsy's perception. The decorum, which subdues Betsy's father and, somewhat less, her brother, enables her to deal with them; but unsubdued masculinity naturally punctures girlish naïveté and brings a mature awareness of sex and death that the girl rejects. Even though she has had to face masculinity in Mr. Speed and death in the loss of her mother, Betsy resists both; thus she has Speed arrested rather than just sending him on his way, and she continues to yearn for her mother's consolation. Her resistance produces her spinsterhood. She also feels betrayal and alienation in the loss of her mother and in her subsequent isolation. She suspects betrayal in the curious male kinship that her father and her brother exhibit with Speed, first in their drinking, second in their sympathy toward him. Her father laments Mr. Speed's arrest: "I regret that the blue coats were called" (166). Though this story came from Taylor's mother, he has clearly made some significant changes in content and character, because the girl of this story is not capable of accepting men, sexuality, and her own maturity. This narrator will die a virgin. And her perpetual virginity leads to the final theme to be discussed, the passage of time.

Regardless of the individual differences of Taylor's best stories, they always deal with decorum or time or both; and when Betsy tries to resist time by clinging to her childhood, she dooms herself to an unfulfilled life. The story suggests that Betsy will turn from greenness to rottenness without the fulfillment of ripe and loving womanhood. Earlier she has tried to escape Mr. Speed by looking into her mirror and saying "away," like Alice in Wonderland, then by having the police remove him. But Mr. Speed, who, in Betsy's ironic words, does turn out to have been "some vague personification of life itself" (161), persists in her memory. The story ends, "It was only the other night that I dreamed I was a little girl on Church Street again and that there was a drunk horse in our yard" (166). She who has rejected the passage of time (and its manifestations, sex and death) has also rejected life.

"The Fancy Woman" (1941)

"The Fancy Woman"[33] was published immediately after "A Spinster's Tale," three months later to be exact, and also concerns sex and a young woman and similar themes; but the differences are more obvious. The spinster begins with a tight-lipped sentence complaining of the drunkenness of her brother and Mr. Speed; in sharp contrast, the third-person narrative voice, which expresses the thoughts of the fancy woman, begins, "He wanted no more of her drunken palaver. Well, sure enough. Sure enough" (167). The narrator of the second story could not be more different from that of the first, and the contrast is no accident. Peter Taylor explained that Robert Lowell, his college roommate, "always teased me about ['A Spinster's Tale'] and he told me that I was prim and puritanical and didn't know anything about the world, that there wasn't enough of the roughness of life in my stories. So I vowed I'd show him, and I sat down and wrote the first sentence of 'The Fancy Woman.'"[34] Taylor added that he had no idea where he was going after that beginning, but he found his way in a different direction with no apparent difficulty. Beneath the pronounced differences of these stories, however, are some remarkable similarities.

Josie, George's kept woman, suffers from none of Betsy's aversions to liquor or men or sex. In fact, she cannot get enough of them; Josie is the opposite side of the coin of sex and alienation. While Betsy suffers from her inability to accept masculine ways and sexual needs (in herself, as well as in men), Josie suffers from her surrendering to her desires for both sex and drink, which leaves her easy prey to men in general and, currently, George in particular. In different ways, men pose overwhelming problems for both women. Furthermore, as each woman suffers, her diction reveals her true nature—Betsy's primness versus Josie's shameless desire, Betsy's pride versus Josie's wish that she had some cause for pride. Though Betsy walls herself off from the world, her alienation brings her a stale safety. Josie's alienation, a far more painful type, arises from her discovery that she is desperately alone in the midst of people. As he does in "A Spinster's Tale," Taylor employs imagery and diction to develop similar themes in "The Fancy Woman."

The story, slanted through the perception of Josie Carlson, shows her precarious relationship with George, who is separated from his wife and who wants to have his fun while protecting his reputation. His answer to the problem is to see Josie discreetly back in Memphis and to take her to his home in the country, where only his closest friends can see her, men who are likely to regard the affair as revenge on his wife and as a display of enviable boldness. Josie has no chance of tying George to marriage, and her week in the country is only meant to placate her for as long as possible. Josie, an alcoholic, vacillates between scheming to marry George and enter the world of wealth and social status, and drinking away her frustrations over what she never can be.

The imagery and diction of the story dramatize the forces Josie contends with. In the second paragraph, stirred from a drunken sleep by "his big hands busying with her clothes, . . . she flung her arms about his neck. And she said, 'You marvelous, fattish thing'" (167). This earthiness and the subsequent mixture of attraction and repulsion, of honesty and pretense, is the foundation of the story, as her first thoughts the following morning indicate: "Damn him! Her blue silk dress was twisted about her body; a thin army blanket covered her lower half" (168). Though she was helpless with drunkenness and desire the night before, she finds in the aftermath that he undressed her only enough for his purposes and left her. Circumstances continue to remind her that physical exploitation is the beginning and end of their relationship, but she grasps for more. Taunting her to ride a horse, he refers to her friends with a lower-class phrase and insults her accidentally. She lashes back: "Friend-girl? You never heard me say friend-girl. What black nigger do you think you're talking down to?" (171). Her very response has the ironic effect of showing her to be the sort of woman she claims not to be. Throughout the story her vulgar language contrasts with her aspirations. She schemes: "He treated her just like the floorwalker at Jobe's the last week she was there. But George was worth getting around [unlike the floorwalker who apparently fired her]. . . . She wouldn't take another drink. She'd find out what was wrong inside him. . . . Little Josephine would make a place for herself at last" (175).

As if to demonstrate the futility of her hopes, some of George's friends come to visit, and Josie observes every detail of these "Mem-

phis society people," the women's "soft skin and natural-colored hair
. . . and shaved legs" (179), their grooming, their clothes of seer-
sucker, linen, and silk. "She wanted to think of herself as like them
. . . thinking that this was the beginning of the new life" (181). But
even though she bathes all the more carefully and continues to dress
in silk, they snub her. She cannot bridge the gap between her com-
monness and their elegance. The morning after a drunken evening
with the society people, she fumes to herself: "'They're none of 'em
any better than niggers. I knew they couldn't be. Nobody is. By God,
nobody's better than I am. . . .' There was no such thing as what these
niggers and whites liked to pretend they were. She was going to let up
and do things in secret. Try to look like an angel. It wouldn't be as
hard since there was no such thing" (185–86).

By virtue of point of view, Josie's emotions serve as the stage where
the conflicts of the story appear. Her nature is to be honest; her need
is to be accepted; her solution is to decide that the aristocracy is all
fake and that all she must do is pretend to be what she is not, just as
society people do; her curse is that she cannot maintain "a little pretense of her own and make a good thing out of old Georgie" (189).

When George's fourteen-year-old son, attracted by her sensuality,
asks to draw Josie, she makes the mistake of responding to the deeper
suggestions of his request and asks, "Clothes and all, Bud . . .?" (197).
He becomes indignant and calls her a "nasty thing," and she realizes
that she has sealed her doom with her suggestive response. Even
though we have reason to believe that Buddy, who has quoted a poem
calling her "the queen of pleasure," would like to seduce her, he will
not admit his desire outright to her or even to himself. The irony of
the experience dawns on Josie in a crushing epiphany: only those who
can play acceptable roles despite what they really feel can achieve or
hold social status. Thus her references to George as a "floorwalker"
show how well he can convey a dignified image and play the proper
role, like Josie's boss, the floorwalker at Jobe's department store. Similarly, she discovers that George's wife, Beatrice, is an actress, showing
that she has mastered her role. With a skill Josie cannot match, Beatrice
already has perfected "a little pretense of her own and [has made] a
good thing out of old George." The central irony of the story is that
Josie, who is neither "nigger" nor "society," is hopelessly caught in
between. She is ill-bred and immoral, but she is also genuine and she
cannot sustain the pretense necessary to rise above her station. She is

wrong in presuming that "there's no such thing" (196) as virtue; but virtue is so far beyond her reach that it does not effectively exist for her.

Though from a very different slant, "The Fancy Woman," like 'A Spinster's Tale," is concerned with themes of decorum, alienation, and the passage of time. While Betsy uses decorum, hides in her alienation, and resists time, Josie never reaches proper behavior, is hopelessly outcast, and yields to time's ravages by abusing liquor and sex. Implicitly, the golden mean of decorous and genuine behavior lies between these extremes, and only in that balance can one live productively.

"The Scoutmaster" (1945)

For the first several pages of "The Scoutmaster"[35] the reader cannot see why Uncle Jake, a family member of no more importance than the others, is the title character. But he personifies a problem that many of the characters face in this complex household where the primary family members—the unnamed boy narrator, Brother, their sister Virginia Ann, and their parents—are joined by Aunt Grace and Uncle Jake. Aunt Grace, newly divorced and twenty-eight years old, stays with her sister and brother-in-law in Nashville for six weeks while rearranging her life and getting a job in Birmingham. Uncle Jake, the brother of the narrator's father, is a permanent member of the household, a widower who has suffered the additional shock of having his only daughter die at nineteen. Facing reality is the central problem of these people, and they respond with varying degrees of success.

The story apparently occurs in the 1930s, and the comments of Virginia Ann and her Aunt Grace set the tone early. The girl uses fad expressions of the period, three of which appear in the first five paragraphs. Virginia Ann, a high school junior, uses trendy sayings like, "Don't tell me that, old dear, because is makes me *too* unhappy" (266). Her language is fashionable and superficial, indicating that she is more concerned with finding ways to use cute clichés than with thinking. The logical extension of talk like this is that two adolescents can have a conversation, say virtually nothing, and be considered witty by their peers. Father cannot "abide" such talk, and when Uncle Jake asks him why, he cannot explain. An obvious objection is its silliness. Just as Virginia Ann tends to be flippant because of her stage in life, Aunt Grace tends to be resolutely cheerful. Her response to her unpleasant situation is to remain cheerful and to enjoy and praise her niece and nephews. She handles her sadness over finally leaving them by displaying a "gaiety" that is "convincing and contagious" (269). Later the narrator says that if Aunt Grace had been present when Father discovered Virginia Ann and her boyfriend compromised, Aunt Grace would have smoothed over feelings afterward with the same "exaggerated sort of cheer" (293).

Virginia Ann's adolescent flippancy and Aunt Grace's relentless good cheer are normal, even helpful, responses to reality; but the same urge to gloss over problems has more serious effects in others. Before her own death, Uncle Jake's daughter, Presh, trying to compensate for the loss of her mother, had turned into "a prig and a fanatic" (268) to salve her pain. The narrator's mother accurately notes, "Presh's religious mania, it's always seemed to me . . . began as very much the same sort of thing as Jake's nostalgia" (282). And that nostalgia becomes the focal point of the story, which is filled with loss and death.

The first loss mentioned is Aunt Grace's divorce of her ne'er-do-well husband, Basil. Suffering considerably more, Jake had lost his brother Louis in childhood, then his wife, then his daughter. Added to these deaths, the normal passing of his parents is yet another of his emotional burdens. Jake's response to pain is to escape through nostalgia and idealization. He tells stories of Louis's rare goodness, assures the narrator that the narrator's parents are ideal, just as Jake's own were, and clings to Boy Scout ritual and lofty phrasing with the same "mania" Presh brought to her religion. Father says that Jake is "really incapable of being very realistic about his dealing with people. His real calling, his real profession is, you know, that of the Scoutmaster. It's during those Thursday night meetings with the boys that poor Jake fulfills himself" (281).

This story has little plot because Taylor is more concerned here with developing characters and revealing their attitudes than with posing a strong dramatic conflict. The crisis, then, is a small incident. Father, Mother, Brother, and Uncle Jake have gone to the Thanksgiving football game at Vanderbilt, leaving the narrator to chaperone Virginia Ann and her date, who is supposed to take her to the game. They, however, settle themselves on the sofa and take advantage of their time alone. Meanwhile, the narrator feels the awkwardness of being designated to monitor the two. He knows they are supposed to leave, but he cannot bring himself to interrupt: "But as the temptation to invade their privacy increased, so did my timidity" (290). He decides he is hungry, goes to the ice box, and finds the "heap of dead quail" his uncle had shot that morning. His appetite naturally gone, he is staring at "their bloody, feathery deadness in the same shelf with the respectable skeletons of roast ducks" (290) when he hears Virginia Ann calling for him quietly to find out if he is near and to make sure that he will not disturb her and her boyfriend.

Quite succinctly, Taylor has juxtaposed two natural fears of a child: death and sex, both of which the narrator is really facing for the first time. He solves the first problem by shutting the refrigerator, but where Virginia Ann is concerned, he hesitates. His solution is to go to his room and wait for his parents to return. When Father walks in on the illicit embrace and orders the boy out, the narrator is filled with relief because decorum is restored and this strange new energy has been stifled. The narrator, like Aunt Grace, Virginia Ann, and Uncle Jake, has now had to face a disturbing reality—the graphic presence of sex and death in his home. His avoidance is natural, and the real problem of the story is not in anything done by him, Virginia Ann, or Father.

The problem is in Uncle Jake's response. He has idealized his brother's children, just as he has his dead brother Louis, and the shock of Virginia Ann's normal but improper conduct is too much for him. Ironically, Uncle Jake says in defense of the boyfriend's tardiness before the game, "Well, well . . . customs change. Everything changes" (287). He can say the words, but he cannot accept them. The narrator has balked; Mother and Father face the problem, chastise the boy and girl, and restore order; but Uncle Jake escapes into the ideal. The narrator and Brother go with Uncle Jake to the Scout meeting, where the narrator finds that his friends in their uniforms all look like strangers. This very artificiality, this role-playing and recitation of the Scout's Oath, is what his uncle clings to: "To the exclusion of all the world Uncle Jake was now become a Scoutmaster" (294). He says to the boys what he would have said to Virginia Ann were he capable of confronting reality, and in his speech calls for the boys "to demand a return to the old ways and old teachings everywhere" (295).

Some critics see Taylor lamenting the passing of old ways in his stories, while others see him calling for people to accept necessary change. Uncle Jake is a ludicrous example of what happens to those who can't face the passing of time or any other unpleasant reality. Apparently Jake will never be able to handle unpleasant truths, and his inability to accept change will prevent him from being anything more than an ineffectual leader of boys.

"A Long Fourth" (1946)

Like Uncle Jake, Harriet Wilson insulates herself from unpleasantness, but the wages of her mistake are greater than his. "A Long Fourth"[36] is a third-person narrative set in Nashville during World War II, and the story comes to the reader through the perception of Harriet, a victim of the comforts she has enjoyed. Son, who is to enter the army on July fifth, comes home to visit his parents and his spinster sisters and brings Ann Prewitt, a "friend," with him. Through conversations over the weekend it becomes apparent that Harriet and Sweetheart, her husband who is a doctor, have reared children who have no capacity to love, no more depth of feeling than their flighty mother and comfortable father.

A series of conflicts brings the theme of the story into focus. The first is expressed in the opening sentence with Harriet's persistent, "I'd be happier, Sweetheart, if B. T. were not on the place" (198). B. T., the nephew of the maid Mattie, is Sweetheart's personal favorite, but he is also coarse, foul-smelling, and given to bouts of wenching. Now that he is grown and does not need Mattie's care, Harriet wants to be rid of him and to have in his place what she calls a well-mannered "darkie" who can work outside or inside as she prefers. The second conflict emerges when Mattie, whose B. T. will have to leave to work in an aircraft factory, compares her loss of B. T. to Harriet's loss of Son, which incenses Harriet. She is angry and wounded that anyone could compare her child to that reprobate. The final clash occurs after the Fourth of July party as Son prepares to take Ann to her train. She has been presumed by the family, and especially by Son, to have only an intellectual interest in him, but she announces to him before the others that she loves him. Taken together, these scenes point to the damage done in the Wilson household by raising children without a capacity to love.

The diction and imagery of the story present a comfortable setting, one filled with pleasantness and gracious living. When Harriet complains about B. T., Sweetheart skirts the problem as always by telling her how pretty she is. When she complains that he never compliments

29

her intellect, he reassures her that she is "nobody's fool" (198). She is so susceptible to transparent flattery that this reassurance has "been consolation to her when Sweetheart had prettied her out of some notion" (198). Ironically, the most confrontational thing she ever does is to turn her back to Sweetheart, retreating rather than confronting. She is so pleased with the benefits of his coddling that she cannot see the cost and is unaware that she has given up her will and intellect, often quoting Mama, Sweetheart, or Son to instruct her thirtyish daughters. She lives in a big clapboard house festooned with wisteria, surrounded by oaks and poplars, and set back a quarter of a mile from Franklin Road. The rank odor of B. T. sours her otherwise pleasant, sweet-smelling house, and she wants him out because of his smell and his misconduct.

The solution to her problem is the origin of the second conflict. B. T.'s draft board orders him to work in an aircraft factory, which will get him off the place, but in grief over his leaving, Mattie compares B. T.'s exit to Son's. "Miss Harriet . . . it's like you losin' Mr. Son. B. T. is gwine too" (208). This brings out Harriet's wrath: "How dare you? That will be just exactly enough from you!" Despite the obvious similarity, Harriet resents Mattie's "open comparison of Son's departure to that of the sullen, stinking, thieving, fornicating black B. T." (209). Harriet is utterly devoid of compassion, and her deficiency of feeling is matched by her scant vocabulary. In trying to express her indignation, she calls on "the language and rhetoric of her mother and of the only books with which she had ever had such acquaintance" (209).

In fact, Mattie's well-intended remark has virtually ruined the weekend for Harriet, so unaccustomed is she to facing unpleasant thoughts. Her daughters even imitate her behavior and parrot her sayings to make a good impression on Ann, but further unpleasantness arises at dinner when the girls clash with Ann and Son over race relations. Time and change have invaded even Harriet's house, and she resists: "She wanted to remember how Son and Helena and Kate had been when they were children" (225). Watching and listening, she later makes a painful discovery about her children. "Her girls had never been in love. And it isn't their height, she thought, and it isn't their legs. They're like Son, she thought, and it isn't them" (227).

She is beginning to see that her children's incapacity for love has come from the way she has handled them and the way she herself has responded to others. The following scene makes the same point. Son brings her a drink before the party as she sits at her dressing table, and she hopes for him to tell her "what is in his heart" (229) before he leaves for the army. He tells her nothing, which is precisely what is in his heart. Son leaves her "standing alone," and she becomes numb with shock and disappointment. She, who has lived superficially all these years, is misguided to hope for sincerity or depth now. In this regard, her son is what she had made him. Only at this point does she feel sympathy for Mattie, who is waiting up for B. T. in the fetid room that only a mother could endure. The elemental image of B. T.'s scent is a physical reminder of the genuineness of B. T., Mattie, and their affection. Despite his immoral ways B. T. does get involved and does take and give love, while Son is well-scrubbed and aloof from all genuine feeling, whether toward his mother or toward Ann.

In an unexpected twist, Ann raises the final conflict of the story, saying to the family: "We have had a very beautiful and very Platonic relationship. He has shown marvelous respect for my intelligence and my virtue. And I, alas, have been so vulgar as to fall in love with him" (232). Son is incapable of the very fulfillment his mother wishes for him. Too late, Harriet is learning compassion; going to comfort Mattie and coming as close as she can to apologizing, she finds "that besides the grief and hostility in Mattie's eyes there was an unspeakable loneliness for which she could offer no consolation" (236–37). Harriet is learning what John Berryman labeled in "The Ball Poem" as "the epistemology of loss." Harriet comes to grips with two losses: one is the natural loss of her children to time and growing up, and the other is an unnatural loss, the discovery that she has never had any real closeness to them anyway. "To Harriet it seemed that her children no longer existed" because she is beginning to see how shallow the life of their family has been. The final images of the story reinforce the contrast of Mattie and Harriet. Mattie sits in that shack "for the sole purpose of inhaling the odor in the stifling air of B. T.'s room," but Son has not even left his mother that much. Instead she lies awake in a chill.

In this story comfort is the curse. The Wilson family has relied on decorum to lead comfortable and utterly superficial lives; the result has been a chilling alienation inside and outside the family, and time is finally making the errors clear to Harriet. Taylor involves the reader in the richness of the house by pointing out the things and words that fill its rooms. Having built this lovely world, he shows it disintegrating.

The Middle Period—
Servants in Conflict

Since upper-class Southern whites are the most common subjects of Taylor's stories, black servants are naturally nearby. Often their role is to give the author opportunities for ironic commentary and insight into their employers. Sometimes, however, they are major characters, which is the case in the stories considered in this section. The reader should not assume that because these servants play supporting roles, Taylor considers them lesser human beings. On the contrary, they are well rendered in their own right, and since they are less bound by decorum, they are often sources of truth and common sense.

Like Taylor's upper-class characters, these servants also have to handle the past. "Cookie" is mainly concerned with the clash of truth and decorum, but the other stories, though they treat issues of decorum, go on to show the danger of letting the past dominate the present. In "What You Hear from 'Em?" the power of the past is evident, as old Aunt Munsie lives on the hope of seeing the two white boys she reared return to live in Thornton, Tennessee, permanently. The live-in servants of "Bad Dreams" become frantic to get rid of their new neighbor, a ragged old black man who reminds them of their origins. Like the first three stories, "Two Ladies in Retirement" was collected in *The Widows of Thornton* (1954), and especially like "Cookie," it uses a servant to reveal the serious problems of one whom she serves. "A Friend and Protector," a much later story from *Happy Families Are All Alike* (1959), continues to focus on decorum, the role of the past, and the weaknesses of the ruling class. (Taylor alludes to Tolstoy by using the first line of *Anna Karenina*.) Though the obviously troubled character here is Jesse, Uncle Andrew, his master, turns out to be escaping vicariously through Jesse's animalism. In each instance Taylor has created vivid black characters who give unexpected insights into the whites they serve.

"Cookie" (1948)

With the publication of "Cookie"[37] in the *New Yorker* in 1948, Taylor began his long association with the prestigious magazine. The story consists of a single scene in which Cookie serves supper and responds to the remarks of the doctor and his wife. It begins with the doctor arriving home with twinges of conscience. Though the narrator enters the doctor's thoughts in the first and last paragraphs of the story, the narrative is otherwise presented from a third-person objective point of view, using only dialogue and appearances to suggest deeper conflict and to reveal the theme.

The opening sentence hints at the problem by mentioning that the doctor comes home for supper a few nights a week because pangs of conscience force him to. As soon as the tension is established, however, evening smells and conversation fill the air, and the doctor's mind, thus diverting the reader's attention. In the overly pleasant manner of one making amends, he tells his wife repeatedly, "You're too good to me." His enthusiastic statements of appreciation sound more motivated by guilt than gratitude. His wife and Cookie treat him as the head of the house, but he could not play that role unless they observed decorum and ignored the truth. Provoked by his condescending banter, Cookie nearly accuses him outright of being the philanderer that they all know he is. The impact of the story comes from the dramatic tension between the doctor's swaggering hypocrisy and Cookie's barely restrained truth, and the tension grows as the wife looks on, hoping not to be confronted with problems she has tried not to see.

Their meal is not a communion between husband and wife but the merest formal contact. He does his duty, consoles his wife, keeps up appearances. Just as he carries on about how lavish the meal is, the doctor also makes a show of his indignation when his wife says that the children send only postcards. Ironically, he who betrays her with adultery rails at his children for not writing long letters to their mother. In his every act during the story, he tries to compensate for reality with pleasant appearances.

The doctor continues his performance as the amazed recipient of his wife's kindness:

> "There's not more, surely?"
> She smiled, nodding her head. "Pie."

"No! What kind!"
"I cooked it myself." (286)

He complains of having too much to eat, then in the same breath asks about dessert. His polite flattery and role-playing are overdone, even by the broad standards of the Southern upper class. The doctor's superficial words to his wife and his patronizing of Cookie make him a more repulsive character with each page of the story. Clearly he believes that proper conduct consists of playing one's role to the hilt: appreciative husband, indignant father, paternalistic employer. He proves himself to be equally insensitive to his wife and to Cookie.

He asks Cookie about her "corporosity" and her "ancestors," presuming to dumbfound her and appear witty to his wife. Then he says to himself in the story's only other departure from the objective point of view, "They really eat it up" (287), adding to his sins of superficiality and adultery the sin of blatant racism.

The climax of the story comes when the self-satisfied doctor stumbles onto a sensitive topic. As he tries to rile Cookie by mentioning Dr. Palmer's maid, Hattie, he implicates himself. Cookie says Hattie is a liar who slanders Dr. Palmer and others, and when Cookie's employer questions her further, she says Hattie claims that he and others have met women at Palmer's house. With the doctor's guilty conscience and shallow nature already being established, we know that Hattie's tale is true. Even though she tells the story at her employer's insistence and prefaces it with a disclaimer, she violates decorum by raising an unpleasant truth and following it with a virtual accusation. "Hattie say she *seen* ya! But she's a liar, aint she, Boss-Man?" (289). The wife calls her down and the doctor, threatened, tries to finish Cookie off on the spot: "Oh I suppose you think you'll have to fire her" (209). He expects his wife to take the suggestion as a mandate, but she doesn't. His wife will observe decorum and allow him to hide behind it, but she will not fire Cookie, the truth teller, merely to appease her husband, the liar.

Cookie is chided for her remarks, but she is not fired, and the doctor is going to have to live with the constant unspoken judgment of her glance. Decorum can protect him to some degree, but it will not shield him from censure and the twinges of guilt mentioned at the beginning of the story. He leaves the house, a man "past fifty," whose "light, sure steps" contrast with the "ugly, old voices" (290) of the women he leaves behind. He has said he has to make some house calls, but his leaving ugly, old voices for a car that is "bright and new and luxurious" clearly implies that Hattie was telling the truth.

As long as he plays his role discreetly, decorum will allow him to continue his nightly adventures, but he must face Cookie's stare and the possibility that his wife will eventually confront him. He can have his social position, his wife, and his sexual affairs, but the price will be high. The ultimate irony of the story is that Cookie, who appears as helpless as an impudent child, may win yet. Decorum has been a potent force in Southern society, persisting even when so much has changed since World War II; but when decorum is used to suppress the truth, it has been abused and will finally fail.

"What You Hear from 'Em?" (1951)

Like Cookie, Aunt Munsie in "What You Hear from 'Em?"[38] is presented in terms of her relationship to the white ruling class. Though the former story is filled with tension and irony, Munsie's is not. The conflict for her is not with people but with circumstances, with time itself. She clings to Thad and Will Tolliver long after she has finished rearing them and they have moved away, and she lives for their visits and in the hope that they will move back to Thornton. The title of the story is her persistent question to the particular people who might have news for her. This small, stooped, faded, little old Negro woman, who pulls her slop wagon down the middle of the street, is a quaint and vivid example of the universal tendency of people to cling to the past.

Pulling her slop wagon, "about the size and shape of a coffin, . . . down the center of the street" (236), Aunt Munsie hardly seems typical; but like many effective characters, she is only an exaggeration of the potential in most people. The point of view through which her story is presented is third-person objective. Everything the narrator tells us appears to be general knowledge available to the well-informed of Thornton. Because she is so visible and so single-minded in her questioning, she lends herself to being story material for the townspeople. Her questioning is the only reason she continues to pull her wagon and collect pig slop well into her old age. Very few literary characters, especially those in Taylor's subdued stories, are as outlandishly symbolic as this wizened old woman, pulling what appears to be a coffin directly down the middle of the street and then raising her hand and stopping all traffic. She cannot deny the facts of mortality and change, but she does resist them.

The Short Fiction: A Critical Analysis

Her more practical resistance appears when Thad and Will visit her, ritualistically exchanging modest gifts, bringing their children along to meet her, and listening to her pleas for them to return to Thornton, where she is convinced they belong. But she merely goes through these necessary motions: "All she wanted to hear from *them* was when they were coming back for good" (235). Her life is sustained by leftovers—the slop for her pigs and the bits of news about the men who are virtually her own children. But, much like Miss Emily Grierson in Faulkner's "A Rose for Emily" (one of Taylor's favorite stories), Aunt Munsie is a public institution, one tolerated, cared for, even thought of proudly, by the townspeople. They sympathize with her longing and her eccentricity. Even black citizens can count on some benefits of decorum: "Nobody would have blown a horn at an old colored woman with her slop wagon—nobody but some Yankee stranger or a trifling high-school boy" (237).

But there is more to Aunt Munsie's defiant use of the streets than eccentricity. As cars become more numerous in the small town of Thornton, she is endangering her life. Perhaps she can't have her boys back, but she refuses to yield any more to the passing of time. Walking down the middle of the street pulling her little wagon, she defies change and invites death. Some people warn her from concern, some from anger; but none will change her. Her daughter Crecie, also an old woman, tells Munsie to visit the boys at their homes in Nashville and Memphis, where they are prosperous and comfortable. But Munsie still holds the nineteenth-century view of the boys' father "that nobody was rich who didn't own land, and nobody stayed rich who didn't see after his land firsthand" (243).

For the old woman, place, identity, and purpose in life are inseparable. The climax of the story occurs when Crecie forces her to face how differently the boys see things. Crecie makes her admit that the boys are never coming back permanently, but Munsie knows that she can't visit them. She laments, "A collie dog's a collie dog anyway. But Aunt Munsie, she's just their Aunt Munsie here in Thornton" (249). Her observation reveals more truth than stubbornness. Nowhere else would people tolerate her peculiarities and appreciate her value as they do in the town where she has lived for eighty years. She is clinging to the past to some degree, but she is also expressing the vital role of context and community in one's identity.

The sad part of the story is that her confrontation with Crecie forces her to give up the vain hope of getting the boys back, and the loss of that hope takes the energy from her life. She gives up the slop wagon and her cantankerousness. She yields, relinquishes her pride and individuality. She falls into the role people expect and becomes the amusing old auntie. Like Miss Lenora in her story and Grandfather Manley of "In the Miro District," when she despairs, she falls into a stereotyped role. Obviously, there are worse things than clinging to the past; better to take comfort in the past than in nothing at all.

The story ends on a point of acute irony. Eccentric people usually have good reasons for being the way they are, and they cannot change and please others without betraying themselves. The third-person narrative voice, which speaks for the white people of Thornton, displays no awareness of loss when Aunt Munsie gives up her hope and her eccentric ways. To them she is "like other old darkies" (251) in her last years. They are right, but she was once a fierce individualist with a dream of fulfillment in her old age. Once the dream is gone, all that is left of Aunt Munsie is a stereotypical "old darkie." Taylor directs the theme of the story to the reader, over the head of the unperceptive narrative persona.

"Bad Dreams" (1951)

The past occupies a much different role in "Bad Dreams."[39] In this story, Bert and Emmaline, who have achieved some status as servants in a prosperous St. Louis household, are not comforted by the past but are threatened by it. Instead of trying to hold on, they are trying to forget.

Mr. Tolliver, the head of the house, brings home a ragged old Negro, who is from west Tennessee, like the servants and the Tolliver family. The majority of the narrative is third person, limited to the thoughts of Emmaline, and her resentment of the old man builds the central conflict early in the story. Unlike Aunt Munsie, Bert and Emmaline are pleased with the present, so pleased that the past and future are threats to their happiness. The old man reminds them of who they are and where they started, "all the poverty and nigger life she had known as a girl in Tennessee" (121). Mr. Tolliver moves the man into a vacant room adjacent to their garage apartment: "And this ragged old man was like the old uncles and cousins whom she had learned to despise before she ever left home" (122). Striking a sharp contrast to the old man is Bert, the immaculate butler. Like his wife, he is determined to run off the unwelcome neighbor.

The threat of the future is raised by the couple's four-month-old baby. The child wakes her parents with inexplicable and inconsolable crying, and in their distress they see the old man in the doorway. He enters, takes the baby from her mother, holds her upside down, and shakes her. Having calmed her, he cradles the child, whom he presumes to be male, in his arms and explains: "Bad dreams is all. I reckon he thought the boogeyman was after him" (136). The narrator opens Emmaline's thoughts to us, expressing her fear that Bert's primitive side might be unleashed by grogginess and frustration and that he might attack the old man. But Bert has become his "daytime" self and says: "It just didn't come to us, I reckon. But what could that little baby have to dream about?" (136). The child, like her parents, seems to have been contending with the ambiguous anxiety that something bad can happen, that the contentment of the moment might be unexpectedly destroyed.

Underscoring the theme of nameless fears, the narrator first tells of the bad dream Emmaline had been having when the baby awoke. Then the point of view shifts to omniscient, and we are told that Bert, too, has suffered a bad dream, even that the old man probably has had one as well. Such fears are presented as a universal burden, and the young couple and their child are united with the old man as fellow sufferers. If life is in some ways a series of common fears and worries to be faced, at least the old man has the grace to face bad dreams. The very man who incited their resentment and stirred old fears has freed them to face what they could not admit.

In this story, which begins in resentment and anger, Taylor offers a conclusion wrought by compassion and common sense. Now that they have met the old man and will probably spend some years near him, Bert and Emmaline have less to be wary of from the past and future. A curse has become a blessing.

"Two Ladies in Retirement" (1951)

"Bad Dreams" and "What You Hear from 'Em?" are both marked by unity and simplicity, and, typical of Taylor's ironic style, the implications of these stories reach beyond the central conflicts. The insights offered by Thornton's reaction to Aunt Munsie's change, and by what Bert and Emmaline have learned, can be useful to any perceptive reader. But the essentially simple approach of these stories is not used in "Two Ladies in Retirement,"[40] a complex story told by an omniscient narrator.

The setting of the story is the Tolliver's house in St. Louis, the locale for "Bad Dreams" and many other stories. With some different characters, the play *Tennessee Day in St. Louis* also takes place in this house. By placing his characters outside the South, just as Taylor found himself as a boy, he can emphasize their distinctive Southern qualities. The very fact that living in St. Louis has not changed the way Amy Tolliver treats her servants shows one powerful influence tradition exerts on her.

At first glance, the story does not appear to be anything out of the ordinary. It begins with a description of Miss Betty Pettigru, goes on with some exposition, some colorful quotations, and more exposition. A beginning like that, along with the omniscient narration, could be found in any one of hundreds of stories. The crucial difference—and the ultimate richness of the narrative—comes from the nature of the central conflict. Miss Betty, a cousin who comes from Nashville to live with the Tollivers in St. Louis, finds herself unexpectedly at odds with the cook, Vennie, over the affection of the three Tolliver boys. Still, this situation does not seem remarkable. The complexity and charm of the story grow from the precise rendering of Miss Betty, her cousin "Flo Dear," and Vennie, as each of these apparently different women faces the problem of maintaining her position in the Tolliver household.

Miss Betty had moved from Thornton to Nashville thirty years earlier when her father set out to find her a husband. Being unattractive, however, she found no man. Instead she made a place for herself in Nashville society, where she became shrewd and powerful. In St. Louis, James Tolliver becomes exasperated by her long visits and suggests that she should make them shorter or move in with him. Even though he immediately apologizes, with such people "there was no relenting once such a thing was said" (297). In the Southern tradition, one can't take back a statement. For Miss Betty the strange invitation becomes the perfect excuse to leave the society world and join a family.

Once the exposition is complete, the action of the story begins with the "terrible competition" (299) between Miss Betty and Vennie. Miss Betty's power derives from her daily closeness to the boys and the treats she buys them. Vennie counters with cooking and story telling. Meanwhile, Flo Dear practices "the absorbing interest of her life" (309), blazonry. She researches and paints coats of arms, dealing with the histories of families as opposed to their current crises.

Each woman has certain powers and limitations. The challenge for each is to take full advantage of her potential without violating her proper limits, and this balance is especially delicate for women outside of immediate families in Southern society. Whether they are guests like Miss Betty and Flo Dear or a veteran servant like Vennie, anyone from outside the immediate family who upsets the household must leave. The ladies would leave in deference to decorum, and Vennie would be fired. (Only immediate family can expect to cause turmoil and stay in spite of all gaffes.) Vennie's first ploy is to tell the servants to continue to treat Betty and Flo like guests, a way of reminding them who got there first and who is needed. Betty counters effectively by merely waiting for Vennie to overstep her limits. At this stage the omniscient point of view moves into Flo's mind for crucial insights: "She knew that Vennie would finally be sent away, but Miss Betty's ruin would lie in her very condescension to this struggle" (306).

Flo, the observer, is gifted at maintaining a proper balance. In earlier years, when Betty wanted her to be her confidante, Flo had been warm but reserved: "She simply could not afford the intimacy and dependency that was being asked of her" (309). She had already made an effort to find a fulfilling life, but her husband deserted her after two months. Betty, on the other hand, had found social life safer and more appealing, and apparently had saved herself the risk of rejection. Flo recalls the deathbed lament of Betty's father: "You've expended your time making a place for yourself among strongheaded women while you ought to have been making your place in the heart of some gentle, honest man" (309). Flo reviews the social career of Miss Betty Pettigru, aptly named considering her pettiness: "Something—surely *something*—better than a life of social climbing could be found" (310).

Furthermore, Betty has been ruthless, harming one person and compensating with great kindness to the next: "Surely, in Nashville, Miss Betty's life had been all sin and expiation, but never with a resolution to sin no more" (310). Betty's perception as she thinks back during her conflict with Vennie is quite different: "Her life there [in Nashville] had never in her eyes been one of sin and expiation. It has just been life, plain and simple" (312). But in the clash with Vennie, she sees that she has paid with her soul for the social success she has had, realizing "that every day of her adult life had made her less a woman instead of more a woman" (313).

As events turn out, Vennie seals her own doom by telling the children she thinks their Auntie Bet and Flo Dear should leave. James

Tolliver fires Vennie, but even so, Betty realizes that she has been prepared to attack and discredit Vennie. She realizes how desperate she is for family love, and she resolves to get deeply involved with the Tollivers, not maneuvering as she has for the last thirty years, but being wholly sincere. She decides at the end of the story that she is "here for life," making her first ultimate commitment.

The story concludes with Flo still on the sidelines. She has always kept her distance and has run no risks since her husband deserted her. Vennie exceeds proper limits and brings her own dismissal. Betty stays within the limits but finally feels compassion for Vennie. She has apparently resolved to sin no more in ways that have been natural to her. In deciding that she will stay until she dies, she has placed commitment above game playing. Demonstrating both contrition and a commitment to others, she is on her way to becoming a whole person.

"A Friend and Protector" (1959)

Collected several years later in *Happy Families Are All Alike*, "A Friend and Protector"[41] is entirely different in tone and action from Miss Betty's subdued narrative. Here Taylor presents a grotesque violence that is rare in his fiction, but like the other stories examined in this chapter, this one also gives simultaneous insight into the servant and his master.

Jesse Munroe, like the unnamed old man from Thornton in "Bad Dreams," is a factotum, almost a pet, to his employer, Uncle Andrew. But unlike the gentle old man in "Bad Dreams," Jesse is full of destructive potential. The first-person narrator of the story is the nephew of Jesse's master; the narrator earlier lived in Memphis with Uncle Andrew and Aunt Margaret after his mother died. In the first paragraph of the story, Taylor has the narrator inadvertently state the problem that plagues both Jesse and Uncle Andrew: "The poor fellow was much too humorless and lived too much in the past—or in some other kind of removal from the present" (142). Jesse is out of touch, and he can be—to Uncle Andrew's vicarious delight—primitive and wild.

There appears to be great mutual devotion between the old men. Jesse regales the narrator with the details of how he would mutilate anyone who dared harm Uncle Andrew. He is ardently devoted, an energetic worker, but he occasionally goes on drunken sprees that lead to his violence and arrest. Uncle Andrew's response in kind to Jesse's devotion is to save him from the consequences of his "escapades" by paying for the damage or by using his influence. In a retrograde motion common in Taylor's stories, the narrator fills in Jesse's background before revealing his fate.

Years earlier Jesse had left the country after Uncle Andrew got him a suspended sentence for complicity in a murder. When he arrived in Memphis, he did not leave his master's property for a year. He was "a timid country boy," somewhat of a "puritan," and "old-fashioned" (145). Ironically, after the other Negroes goaded him into going out, he became a drinker and fighter, and eventually a con man, who "specialized, for a time, in preying upon green country boys who had come to Memphis" (155). These boys bore an unmistakable resemblance to the young Jesse, yet they met the old Jesse, with hair "long and brushed up" and "bloodshot eyes," a "fierce-looking" character (143).

Furthermore, when Jesse recites his litany of devotion to Uncle Andrew and tells what he would do to whoever harmed him, he faces his own image in a mirror, "certain to see the black visage of the man he was mutilating" (154). Both his real exploitation of the country boys and his imagined mutilations are attacks on surrogates of himself.

From a psychopathological standpoint, Jesse's conduct makes sense: he is attacking himself. His drunken sprees, fights, and inevitable disgrace feed his need to debase himself. The most important by-product of Jesse's misconduct—perhaps even its true purpose—is to cause Uncle Andrew to intervene and make expiation. The escapades grow "successively worse," and Uncle Andrew's intervention each time gives Jesse "considerable satisfaction" (149). On the one hand, he is self-destructive and feels guilty and unworthy; on the other hand, he craves proof of his worth. Jesse, then, exhibits a divided self and divided urges.

The story is built on a pattern of doubles. In a somewhat similar manner, Uncle Andrew is also divided. The major difference is that Jesse acts out both his social and his antisocial natures. Uncle Andrew plays the social role and uses Jesse as a vicarious expression of his suppressed violence, like the Victorian Englishmen who were avid fans of dog fights and cock fights. Since he lacks the courage or energy to express his aggression, he uses Jesse. The final irony is that the "friend and protector" has been the unwitting exploiter.

The story concludes in an epiphany. Jesse has gotten into trouble for fraud and procuring and has had to go into seclusion again, as he did when he arrived in the city years before. This time, however, he stays in Uncle Andrew's cotton warehouse, and this time his spree consists of getting drunk and wrecking Uncle Andrew's office. His excesses have destroyed him, and he is committed to an asylum, but as the narrator observes: "This was not merely the story of that purplish-black, kinky-headed Jesse's ruined life. It is the story of my aunt's pathetically unruined life, and my uncle's too, and even my own. . . . I understood that Jesse's outside activities had been not only *his*, but *ours* too. . . . [My aunt and uncle] forced Jesse's destruction upon him . . . because they were so dissatisfied with the pale *unruin* of their own lives" (160).

Much earlier in the story, the narrator has provided subtle evidence of how he also savors Jesse's violent actions. He explains Jesse's involvement in the disposal of a murdered man's body, which was dismembered. The narrator confesses: "You may wonder why I bring in these awful details of the murder, and I wonder myself. I tell them out of some kind of compulsion" (150). It is the compulsion of one who enjoys, but will not take part in, the violence of others.

The uncle, and even his wife, draw a certain vitality from Jesse's wildness. He serves as an alter ego to vent their passions, but he goes too far with his final drunken frenzy. The doubling effect is no longer useful, and they have him committed because he becomes more of a threat than an outlet. The behavior that appears generous throughout the story is only self-serving. Uncle Andrew and Jesse ironically bring out the worst in each other.

The conflicts in these stories, whether they come from the society at large, the white employers in particular, or the servants themselves, lead the reader to a deeper understanding of servants and masters. Sometimes more than they realize or would ever wish, the blacks and whites in Taylor's fiction have lives that are inextricably involved. The involvement is not vaguely societal but personal and profound.

The Middle Period— Self-discoveries

From later in the middle period of Peter Taylor's short fiction come several stories that examine characters trying to understand themselves. Sometimes they tell of their own experiences and sometimes of people whom they have watched since childhood; other times a third-person narrator reveals the characters. The autobiographical "1939" and *"Je Suis Perdu"* make a natural pair, being portraits of the artist at the beginning and middle stages of his career. In these stories the social context is merely a useful backdrop, while in the others of this period the expectations of society exert a decisive influence on the action. "Venus, Cupid, Folly and Time" and "Guests" both deal with old couples clinging to familiar social forms and resisting the passage of time. Though the couples and their behavior are different, all of the old people display eccentric behavior that they consider natural. "The Other Times" and "Miss Lenora When Last Seen" resound with the ironic hollowness of superficial behavior. Both stories present a narrator who has the perception to appreciate the courage of others but lacks the strength to take similar risks.

In the stories considered in this section, the interplay of social form and individual will leads characters to the brink of self-discovery. The first five stories were originally collected in *Happy Families Are All Alike*, and "Miss Lenora When Last Seen" is the title story in Taylor's next collection. The first two stories reveal a writer, who, first in youth then in middle age, makes important self-discoveries. The remaining stories set forth either a protagonist or a narrator who comes to the verge of insight into himself but stops there, unable or unwilling to confront unpleasant truth. They hide behind conventional attitudes or social forms. In these stories Taylor elaborates on the vices and virtues of decorum.

The Growth of the Artist:
"1939" (1955) and *"Je Suis Perdu"* (1958)

Even though "1939"[42] was published in 1955, the first-person narrator begins, "Twenty years ago, in 1939 . . .," and then he quickly sets the mood for this reminiscence—"restless and uneasy" (326). Aside from this slight tinkering with dates and the necessary fictional names, this story is full of autobiographical fact. Of course there is nothing new about autobiography in fiction, but in Taylor's work it is usually much more subdued. Here, however, the author addresses us essentially as himself, perhaps because the boys of the story seem so dear and remote to him. Full of youthful ambition and frustration, they are so distant in time and mood that they constitute a fictional world of their own.

The narrator never gives his name, but he and his roommate Jim Prewitt are both seniors at Kenyon College. Like Taylor and his roommate Robert Lowell, who had achieved considerable success as a poet by the time this story appeared, the boys live in an old house set aside to accommodate transfer students. They and the other residents of the house "had all come to Kenyon because we were bent upon becoming writers" and they followed a "distinguished poet" (334) to the small college. Taylor and Lowell met at Vanderbilt, where Lowell had transferred from Harvard expressly to study under John Crowe Ransom, the poet and professor in the story. When Ransom moved to Kenyon in 1937, Lowell made a second transfer to follow him; Taylor dropped out of school for a year, then joined the others at Kenyon in 1938.

When Lowell read this story in 1955, he was moved to anger, then envy, and wrote to Taylor, with whom he maintained a lifelong friendship. "*At first I was, how shall I put it, surprised and hurt* . . . but since then I have [had] so many compliments—nothing I have ever written myself has ever gotten me such attention. . . . [I] thank you with grudging bewildered incomprehension. But were we really quite such monsters?"[43]

In the middle of the story the narrator addresses his reader directly and makes a defense of basing his story on fact:

> Before seeing me again in the car that November night in 1939, picture me for just a moment—much changed in appearance and looking at you through gold-rimmed spectacles—behind the lectern in a classroom. I stand before the class as a kind of journeyman

writer, a type of whom Trollope might have approved, but one who has known neither the financial success of the facile Harvard boy [who became a wealthy Hollywood scriptwriter] nor the reputation of Carol Crawford [based on Jean Stafford]. Yet this man behind the lectern is a man who seems happy in the knowledge that he knows— or thinks he knows—what he is about. And from behind his lectern he is saying that any story that is written in the form of a memoir should give offense to no one, because before a writer can make a person he has known fit into such a story—or any story, for that matter—he must do more than change the real name of that person. He must inevitably do such violence to that person's character that the so-called original is forever lost to the story. (339)

In the manner of Trollope himself, Taylor turns to his reader and tells him what he hopes to do. He raises three points that bear on the whole story. First, just as the narrator expected and dreaded in 1939, he has not won the money or reputation he had hoped for. Second, in telling this story he now "thinks he knows" what he wants to achieve. Third, the "so-called original" cannot be precisely reproduced in the story—*so-called* suggesting that our memories always modify the original details anyway. The passage quoted above is a digression, but by this point in the story digressions have become common. Comments that appear superfluous contain the truth of the story, which the narrator "thinks he knows" how to reveal by means of digression.

The overt action of the story is a trip that the boys make from Ohio to New York City over the Thanksgiving weekend. But the physical action is, appropriately, circular because the important movement and conflict occur within the boys. They do drive to New York and meet girls they know, go on to see Jim's parents in Boston, then take a train back to Ohio. The scenes with the girls are full of an uneasiness that has dramatic value. Most of the story, however, is not devoted to narrative but to the passionate observations and aspirations that the narrator recalls from his restless final year in college. Taylor wrote fifteen pages before he got down to the apparent story: what happened in New York. The truth of "1939" lies not in facts, but in feeling, in the mood. Creating that mood is the purpose of the story, and digression is his method.

The overt conflicts stir the narrator and move him toward subtler, more important, struggles. He and all his friends reject fraternity life, represented by the fraternity boys who parade along the Middle Path and sing in the evenings: "For us, the Middle Path was the epitome of everything about Kenyon that we wanted no part of" (333). They refuse to enter into what they consider the mindless jocularity of college social life. They presume such happiness to be the effect of wealth and privilege, so when they observe tramps beyond the campus, who also seem happy, they do not know what to think.

The narrator recalls ironically that he and his literary friends went on long walks through the country and talked at length of the books they had read, "but I think none of us ever listened to anyone's talk but his own" (335). To his surprise he recalls "how happy those tramps seemed. And how sad and serious we were" (336). The joy of the tramps and of the fraternity boys comes from their unself-conscious, relaxed state. But the young apprentice writers, painfully aware of their individual differences and grappling with serious questions, cannot achieve the peace that the rich and poor on either side of them can.

The surface conflict of the story is with the girls. The immediate problem comes from the boys' confusion of the ideal with the real: "Each of us carried in his mind an image of the girl who had inspired him to make this journey" (337). Anyone who starts out like this is bound for disappointment, but the girls raise further complications. Nancy, the narrator's girl, has already dropped him for another boy, and Carol, Jim's girl, drops him in favor of her growing career as a writer. (Carol is based on Jean Stafford, who did have early literary success but also married Lowell.)

Beneath the boys' image of the girls, and the disappointment they find in New York, is the dominant force in the story—their image of themselves. En route to New York the narrator has a revealing sensation.

> And in my mind's eye I saw the other Douglass House boys—all seven of them—still lingering on the stone steps of the front stoop, leaning against the iron railing and against one another, staring after us. But more than that, after the image had gone I realized suddenly that I had pictured not seven but *nine* figures there before the house, and that among other faces I had glimpsed my own face and that of Jim Prewitt. It seemed to me that we had been staring after ourselves with the same fixed, brooding expression that I saw in the eyes of the other boys. (340)

Symbolically, the trip to New York is an excursion into maturity, a trial run as it turns out, and the narrator watches himself the whole time. At the time he even wears his "first mustache" (341), another obvious mark of trying to grow up and leave boyhood behind. Nancy's response is to tell him to "shave that fuzz off your lip" (341). This girl gives no quarter to the delicate ego of a young man. Before their time in New York is over, the boys both suffer "a mixture of anger and humiliation" (344) at the girls' hands. True to their vocation, both boys lose themselves in writing on the return trip by train; but instead of calming them, their writing disturbs them more. The narrator's fiction and Prewitt's poetry become vehicles of competition between the two. Finally they end up shoving each other around an empty smoking car to vent their frustration.

What causes so much tension? The girls are not the real problem. At the bottom of their turmoil is the feeling that they have taken a turn at adult life and failed. The girls have rejected them, they do not know how to act in strange surroundings, and they are so self-conscious that they are always looking at themselves, like a boy with a mustache, who wonders without uttering the words: *Am I grown yet?* They return to Douglass House, completely at peace with each other after their violence, and they get an answer to the question. Glad to be back and "dead for sleep," the narrator can "hear the train wheels saying *Not yet, not yet, not yet*" (359).

"Je Suis Perdu" is set eighteen years later. The narration has changed from a first-person reminiscence to a third-person account of recent events. The writer in "1939" can comfort himself by thinking "not yet"; that is, *I don't have to grow up yet.* There is time to enter maturity through more attempts, like the trip to New York. Not so in *"Je Suis Perdu."* The viewpoint character is the writer from "1939," and he is thirty-eight years old, not twenty.

The younger writer suffers the anxiety and folly of youth, but he also feels a consoling sense of the possibilities ahead of him. The older writer is "only thirty-eight. But the bad thought was that he was no longer *going to be* this or that. *He was.* It was a matter of *being.* And to *be* meant, or seemed to mean at such a moment, to *be over with*" (497). His life has gone well. He has rich rewards of a wife and children and a satisfying career. His only cause for regret is that becoming has given way, inevitably, to being.

Whereas "1939" establishes and elaborates on a single mood, this story is built on opposing moods. The first is expressed in the writer's response to the antics of his well-coordinated infant son: "What a lucky break!" (491). This year, now ending as they prepare to leave Paris and return to the United States, has been ideal. His writing, their living conditions, the progress of their children—all have been ideal. The simple problem is that the year must end. "He *was*." As surely as *was* carries a sense of mortality when it is used so pointedly by Faulkner in *The Sound and the Fury,* it is also the death knell of this man's youth.

In both of these stories the primary conflict is within a character, and his mixed feelings are even presented with a lightly ironic touch that jests at the man's exaggerated self-pity. But knowing that he has no real justification for his sadness does not make the feeling disappear. The conflict of the later story is even represented with an allusion to Milton. Taylor entitles the two sections *"L'Allegro"* ("the cheerful man") and *"Il Penseroso"* ("the pensive man"), displaying an ironic self-mockery that keeps the story light without diminishing the weight of his autobiographical character's emotion.

The writer starts out by resolving to shave off the mustache he has had for this year, as if to admit that this ideal, almost frivolous, stage of his life is over. This gesture of acceptance sets him apart from his younger self in "1939." He surrenders his mustache voluntarily. Then what causes his subsequent dread over leaving? The innocent French of his daughter, who spills milk and cries, *"Je regrette"* (492). She says the words, but he realizes that the deeper regret is his.

Her statement causes him to think back to another cry in French that surprised him. Separated from her father in an exiting movie crowd, she yelled, *"Je suis perdue!"* (493). But she was lost only for the moment. Now he fears that he is lost—at least his youth is lost—forever. His daughter, speaking French much better than he, and with her life still before her, has innocently caused "chilling sensations" in her father, and *"L'Allegro"* draws to a close.

In *"Il Penseroso"* he wonders why his good mood has disappeared. Then when his daughter hugs him later and dispels the sadness that seems so powerful and even philosophically appropriate, he begins "to feel resentful again of the interruption and of the mysterious power she had over him" (501). He feels "cheated," as if, Taylor suggests with thoroughgoing self-mockery, a writer should be allowed to make the most of his depressions. This is not William Faulkner's sort of response to mortality, considering the desperate acts of the Compson family in *The Sound and the Fury,* but it is Peter Taylor's.

The conclusion is surprising and altogether right. The writer admits within himself, and on the verge of laughter, that there are "ideas and

truths and work and people that he love[s] better even than himself"
(501). A child's hug has utterly vanquished a man's depression, and
the writer, in spite of himself, is redeemed.

Observations of the Old Order: "Guests" (1959) and "Venus, Cupid, Folly and Time" (1958)

Perhaps the chief benefit of decorum in daily life is that it dictates the
proper behavior in difficult situations. Tradition sometimes sustains
people, especially Southerners, when individual strength or faith is
weak. The youthful, then middle-aged, writer in the stories above has
to deal with time and change but never in the severe terms of the old
people in "Guests" and "Venus, Cupid, Folly and Time."[44] The writer
has consolations that these people do not: in youth he has hope, and
in middle age he has his children—hope made flesh. For better or
worse, the main characters of "Guests" and "Venus, Cupid, Folly and
Time" rely on their notion of proper behavior to face or resist old age
and death.

In "Guests" Taylor focuses on Johnny and Annie Kincaid, the country cousins visiting Edmund and Henrietta Harper, but the action of
the story finally reveals both couples. The third-person-limited point
of view is slanted through Edmund, which delays our perception of the
dominance of the women over their husbands. The story begins with
a comic-pathetic tone. The country cousins try so hard to cause no
inconvenience that their very efforts are disturbing. If they were not
trying to be so considerate, they would be easier to deal with. Henrietta, on the other hand, is a compulsive hostess who, for twenty-five
years, has been assisting with and meddling in the lives of her invited
relatives. Edmund has endured his wife's efforts with tolerance and
even amusement. The story, then, has considerable comic potential,
but Taylor chooses, finally, to overrule comedy with tragedy.

Henrietta, who is childless and urban, offers her relatives a hospital-
ity that has been of little benefit: her "nieces had eloped . . . nephews
had taken to a wild life" and "convalescents always outstayed their
welcome" (409). The ones she most wants to stay with her are the
young and healthy, who need her the least. Taylor makes clear what
Edmund should know: that Henrietta is a sadly barren woman, as
much so emotionally as physically.

Edmund and Henrietta are fifty-eight years old; thus her "projects"
began at about the same time she would have concluded that she could

not have children: twenty-five years ago, when she was thirty-three. Since that point in her life, she has substituted guests for children. She wants to fill her life with the vitality of her guests; therefore, she has no use for the sick and hurries them off. The comfort she is primarily concerned with is her own.

From the beginning we see the benign conflict between the Harpers' expectations and the Kincaids' country ways. But there is no harm done by a difference of habits. The harm comes from the war of wills that develops between Henrietta and Annie. Under the excuse of courtesy Henrietta tries to dominate the lives of the Kincaids. Annie maintains her pride and autonomy by being careful not to impose.

They even use their husbands as means of attacking each other with volleys of politeness. The first skirmish is Annie's refusal to tell Henrietta what foods Johnny cannot eat. If the hostess does not know, she cannot go to extra trouble and put them deeper in her debt. The result is that Annie's pride is spared at the expense of Johnny's health. Edmund grasps what is going on: "Edmund had thought of Cousin Annie as waging a merely defensive war against Henrietta. Now he saw it wasn't so. She had the offensive from the beginning and she was winning battle after battle. Every discomfort that Johnny suffered in silence . . . was a victory over Henrietta" (430).

The end of the war between the women comes with Johnny's death during the night. At first, through Edmund's perception, it appears as though Annie would risk her husband's death rather than upset her hosts by calling a doctor. In the morning Annie explains that he had been near death when they came but that he wanted to see the city. She humored him by consenting to a trip to Nashville, but she would not surrender her pride; thus, "Edmund detected the glint of victory in the last glance she gave Henrietta" (435). She has at least presided over the death of her husband in country fashion. Edmund muses, "Annie didn't realize you couldn't die without a doctor nowadays" (436).

The more Edmund considers the events, the more he sees that Annie's war was not offensive. It was defensive, if it was a war at all. At the request of her dying husband, she consented to leave the security of her home and visit Nashville. She further yielded to his wishes by letting him go as far and do as much as he was able to do. Faced with her husband's imminent death in a strange house, she did the best she could to preserve his independence and dignity. After all, everybody from the country knows that people should die at home. In his thought that people can no longer die without a doctor, Edmund delivers a telling satiric blow to modern life, city life, and the assumptions that modern urban people live by. Annie's code is an old and venerable one, and it shows more common sense than Edmund's. Johnny died without a doctor, not because of Annie's perverse pride, but because it was time for him to die, and Annie had sense enough to see that. I suggest that the "glint of victory" (435) in Annie's eye is only imagined by Edmund. The glint is more likely caused by emotional strain and the effort to hold back tears.

Much earlier in the story Edmund thinks of Johnny, "Here is such a person as I might have been, and I am such a one as he might have been" (423). At the end of the story he returns to this thought. Except for his moving from the country years ago, he might be just the kind of man Johnny was. He is sad that he and the old man never talked freely to each other, but he finally realizes that each has been "lost" without his "old realities."

The clash of their wives over matters of decorum has occupied center stage in this story, but the overshadowing problem of the story appears at the end. Decorum has become so vital to all of these people because their world has changed, and they need a frame of reference to govern their conduct. Edmund addresses Johnny's corpse: "The country wasn't itself anymore. . . . By 'country' we mean the old world, don't we, Cousin Johnny—the old ways, the old life, where people had real grandfathers and real children, and where love was something that could endure the light of day. . . . Our trouble was, Cousin Johnny, we were lost without our old realities" (437). At the beginning of the story decorum is a matter of table manners. By the end it becomes a matter of moral philosophy, of epistemology and ethics. Decorum is the old reality without which the new generation is lost.

Although "Guests" is nearly over before Edmund Harper discovers the significance of Johnny Kincaid's decline and death, he does reach an epiphany. In "Venus, Cupid, Folly and Time" Taylor employs a first-person-plural narrator that narrows in the last three pages to the voice of a single unnamed speaker, and neither the group he represents, nor the individual narrator ever understands the story. Taylor employs an irony that requires readers to work in partnership with him in order to grasp truths that the narrator utterly misses.

The Kincaids in "Guests" are in most ways ordinary people for their time and place. Their pride is typical, even though extreme. Louisa and Alfred Dorset also have their pride and want to hold onto their "old realities," but they surpass the proud reserve of the Kincaids and become notorious eccentrics. The collective narrator says that their bizarre behavior "disturbed and annoyed" everyone. They are oblivious to their neighbors. In their reckless determination to halt the passage of time, they resemble Miss Emily Grierson, the protagonist of Faulkner's "A Rose for Emily." Taylor has mentioned this story among his favorites more than once, and "Venus, Cupid, Folly and Time" shows some noteworthy similarities to it in setting, conflict, and theme. The story even uses a "we" narrator like the one that tells Faulkner's tale.

Taylor's first concern in this story is to establish the strangeness of the Dorsets, an unmarried brother and sister fiercely loyal to each other. They draw from the community alternating gusts of pity and revulsion. The narrative enumerates their peculiarities: small things like going downtown still wearing their night clothes under regular clothing, and large things like creating their "curiously mutilated house" (294) in order to save tax money.

Only after acquainting us with the eccentricities of the old couple does the narrator give us some surprising news: these weird people are "despite everything . . . social arbiters" (295), solely because they give an "annual dancing party" for the select young people of Chatham (Taylor's fictitious representative Southern city). For reasons difficult to explain, the party has become a rite of passage for upper-class teenagers: "Sensible parents wished to keep their children away. Yet what could they do?" (296). The Dorsets, who disregard and even attack conventional behavior, have become an institution, and their party is protected by tradition. Well-bred boys and girls have always gone to the party. Why? There appear to be two major reasons for the status of their party. First, the Dorsets are the last remaining descendants of one of Chatham's founding families. The others moved on when they found better opportunities. Second, the party itself is such a grotesque display that the experience of attending it is irresistible.

Like Miss Emily, the Dorsets themselves, their house, and even their fabled annual party, are grotesque. Like her, they wage a pathetic but spirited battle with time. Like her—and everyone else—they lose the battle. Like her, they are used by their creator to show that the community is as flawed as they are. In both stories the townspeople refuse to see something that is upsetting. In Emily's case, they refuse to link the disappearance of Homer Barron with the foul smell that rises from her house. In the Dorsets' case, there is nothing so serious as murder, but there are strange things: for example, Miss Louisa's housecleaning in the nude. What is the community's response? "Some neighbors got so they would not even admit to themselves what they saw" (291). Certainly the Dorsets have done nothing criminal, and they are entitled to their privacy and their weirdness. But at least people could be honest about what they see.

Readers who want to take Peter Taylor as a mourner of the Old South, as another Southern writer who wishes the past could come back, can read this story and learn otherwise. Certainly he does evoke the charms of the past in many of his stories, but longing for the past is never a solution to the troubles of the present. Those who try to hold onto the past in his stories are always absurd to some extent, and the Dorsets are the outer limit of absurdity in Taylor's work.

Before the ill-fated party takes place, Taylor has prepared us to see the weaknesses of the older and younger generations. Everyone who goes to the Dorsets' house has seen that the third story and a whole wing of the house have been torn away. The Dorsets' choice, as they saw it, was to leave each other and live with relatives or to sacrifice their house, save money on taxes, and remain there. Their decision has resulted in the grand but ludicrous gesture of dismembering their home. Of course, the gesture is symbolic as well as practical. They have, as they are wont to say, "given up everything for each other" (295).

Legend has also warned the young guests of what to expect inside the house: "a strange perfume" smelling like "a mixture of spicy incense and sweet attar of roses," curious indirect lighting, and representations of Rodin's *The Kiss*, of Leda falling prey to the swan, and of Bronzino's painting "Venus, Cupid, Folly and Time" (298–99). Add to this rather erotic atmosphere an old maid and an old bachelor, each coated with "suntan powder" and tinged with rouge, and you have the scene that each child entered, year after year. This is not the sort of place where a parent likes to think of his child spending the evening.

But the parents of Chatham have found a solution: they refuse to think. The parents of Ned and Emily Meriwether (who are later cast into a frightening parallel to the Dorsets) discuss their misgivings, and Mrs. Meriwether complains, "But we *can't* keep them away" (302). Of course they can. They just lack the character to resist tradition and swim against the tide of fashion. When they hear unexplained noises downstairs, after the children are supposed to be gone, they explain them away and go on "talking and deceiving themselves" (302). With the Dorsets on one side, buried in the past, and the parents on the other side, numb in the present, what chance do children like the Meriwethers have to be reasonable and sensitive?

In the dark subsurface of this story, the imagery and dialogue imply incest, or at least the potential for it. At the party the Dorsets lead the children around their house, explain its history and deliberate partial destruction, trying to express what they value: "As though money ever took the place . . . of living with your own kind. . . . Or of being well born" (306–7). After this speech they launch into their famous solo dance, and the children watch as the old people wilt. After their dance, Mr. Alfred, "in the dark, flower-bedecked downstairs hall," proclaims, "And love can make us all young forever" (308). He adds, "Remember what our life is like here!" His sister brings the story to an intermediate climax when she adds passionately, "This is what it is like to be young forever!" (309).

Meanwhile, the Meriwether children have gotten their low-born friend, Tom Bascomb, in without an invitation in order to mock the Dorsets. Soon after the Dorsets finish rhapsodizing, Tom, pretending to be Ned Meriwether, starts kissing Emily Meriwether, and everyone laughs at the prank played at the Dorsets' expense. But Ned, to his own surprise, does not laugh. He appears to be jealous and then to be embarrassed over the incestuous implications of that jealousy. To his dismay he recognizes the potential in all of us to become like these pitiable old people.

In another similarity to "A Rose for Emily," Taylor's story ends with parents invading the house of the misfits who have tried to stop time. Though Faulkner's story ends with the actual death of his grotesque Emily Grierson, Taylor's ends with the figurative death of the Dorsets—the end of their traditional parties. When the parents enter the house to take their children home, the Dorsets are upstairs, more alienated than ever. For without their illusion that they can resist time and prove their triumph over it with these parties, they die emotionally, as Miss Emily died literally.

Speaking to Mrs. Meriwether, Mr. Dorset insists that he could tell that Tom was an interloper. He clings to his belief in appearances and a caste system: "People *are* different" (319). The sad irony is that he is sure Ned, and not Tom, is the low-born boy. The Dorsets have sustained themselves for years on the power of their illusions, but the irreverence of their detractors can be just as dangerous.

The final ironic twist is that the night has had such a powerful effect on the Meriwether family: the parents send Ned and Emily off to school and the children are never close again. The Dorsets have lived on brittle illusions and have an unhealthy, if not perverse, relationship, but their devotion is noble. At the end of the story the narrator tries to explain to an outsider why the story of the Dorset family matters: "If the distinction [between founding aristocrats and upstarts] was false, it mattered all the more and it was all the more necessary to make it" (323). However sad and misguided the Dorsets may be, they pursue an ideal, which is more than Taylor can say for the new generation.

The Kincaids and the Dorsets are, in different ways, ludicrous couples, but they do possess an odd nobility. In spite of everything, they hold onto what they value. A natural tendency might be for a reader to conclude that Taylor is mourning the passing of the Old South, but such a conclusion would be a mistake. These old people never transcend their desperate attachment to their old identity and old ways; thus their creator is not holding them up as heroes. He is only saying that the old must pass; but the new generation, which has the opportunity to live in the present, is not offering any improvements. The old have illusions; the new have indifference to matters of family and decorum. These are misguided extremes, and by implication, the proper course to travel is a middle ground that few of Taylor's characters find: the solid footing of veneration for the past, mixed with acceptance of the present.

The Triumph of Hollowness: "The Other Times" (1957) and "Miss Lenora When Last Seen" (1960)

"The Other Times"[45] is told by a first-person narrator reflecting on events of roughly twenty years before. Many elements in the story anticipate "The Old Forest," a story published twenty-two years later. Notably, the action in "The Old Forest" is presented by a narrator recalling what happened forty years earlier. Both stories have major characters named Ramsey, both deal with the delicate social issue of boys moving in two different social realms, both use the same speakeasy tavern, and both involve an upper-class girl in a social crisis. In "The Old Forest" the girl takes charge and resolves the crisis, but in "The Other Times" a man takes control by sacrificing himself.

The story is built on social tension. The narrator, who admits to having been "a worrier" (107), recalls the awkward situation of the upper-class girl, the kind who will "make her debut some day" at the country club (81). The lovely Letitia Ramsey faces what the narrator considers the grave embarrassment of having an uncle who is a high school civics teacher. Louis Ramsey is a civics teacher and baseball coach, the sort of job notorious for attracting the rough, inarticulate man who can't stand to leave the adolescent joy of sports.

By his manner and chosen profession, Louis has renounced his aristocratic birthright. He is a "hard drinker and a general hell-raiser" (81), and his niece and her family are the opposite. Letitia, nevertheless, is fond of him and is never embarrassed as the narrator keeps expecting her to be. Unlike her girlfriends with peculiar relatives, she never apologizes for him. Thus the tension of the story comes from within the narrator himself. He reflects the conventional attitude that decent people must be "pretty careful not to mix" (87) upper-class and lower-class activities. But this same boy cannot resist the adventure of taking Letitia to an illegal roadhouse. Earlier in the story, only Louis Ramsey's presence raises a conflict. From this point on, conflict fills the story, and imagery underscores the disturbance.

Three couples choose to leave the sedate elegance of Nancy O'Connor's lawn party and go to Aunt Martha's Tavern. The lawn party is held in a walled yard with Japanese lanterns, and Nancy's bizarre, unspeaking grandmother lurks in the shadows watching the boys and girls. In her black dress, says the narrator, the old woman "might easily have been mistaken for a Catholic nun" (88). She is an apt symbol of strict propriety. Soon they are being observed by other equally disturbing creatures: the stuffed animals that are hung around the walls of the tavern. As all of the imagery indicates, they have gone from proper to improper surroundings, from the societal world to the animal world. The narrator mentions the "creepy sight" of the other boys and girls "coming out of the woods" after the raid (104). Social forces have subdued the animal impulses to carouse and dance, but only temporarily.

Taken symbolically, the scene can represent the conflict of the narrator's superego and id. Though the narrator goes to the tavern, he is more comfortable in the gaze of the grandmother than before the glass eyes of stuffed animals. He is more at ease in a social setting than in a primitive one. When Aunt Martha banters with the boys, she calls them "jelly beans" (92), a slang term that has disappeared from the language. Loosely it means "dandies" or "the pampered," which applies to them but not to Louis Ramsey.

Louis is coarse but genuine, and he represents the vitality that comes from directness and simplicity. He lacks social grace, but he also lacks the weakness and indecisiveness that plague the narrator, a confessed "worrier." Louis does not worry; he acts. He decides to sacrifice himself to the arresting officers in order to make sure that Letitia is not discovered. When Louis sees Letitia to safety, the narrator refers to "that look" of hers that expresses "the beautiful confidence she had in him all because he was an uncle of hers, I suppose" (100).

At the end of the story he says, "I was really wishing that I knew how to make a girl like her look at me that trusting way, instead of the way she had been looking at me earlier" (107). Here Taylor offers us, through an unperceptive narrator, the crux of the story. Letitia does look at him before they enter the tavern. As he attempts to "steal a quick glance at her" (89), he discovers that she is already looking at him, as if hoping for something. That look appears to be the natural precursor of the look she gives her uncle. Even though she is proper, she looks directly at him: "She kept right on looking without changing expressions." She is being genuine, direct like her uncle and hoping for the same from the narrator.

Her look at Louis has nothing to do with his being her uncle; rather it is her natural response to the genuineness and courage of her uncle's action. What the imagery and action of the story show is that the narrator is afraid of taking a chance. He cannot see that Letitia's look could just as well have been for him. She is not looking for a bold knight, just for a boy with enough courage to act and take consequences. After that night he will not even ask her out until after his summer trip abroad. He explains, "I didn't want her to think I was trying to make something out of our happening to be put together that night" (105). But why shouldn't he? They just went through a frightening experience together and witnessed the ruin of her uncle's coaching career. He should "make something out of" the experience but will not because he fears involvement.

At the end of the story he brings forth a question from those days, a question that he apparently cannot answer now any better than then. "But the point is I *didn't* know how to make a girl like her look at me that way. And the question is why *didn't* I know how?" (107). The way is to be genuine, to act, even to act recklessly if the situation requires.

What he does not see—and what Taylor tells us through dramatic irony—is that one cannot be safe and fully alive at the same time.

Final proof comes in the last paragraph of the story when he mentions seeing "someone like Letitia nowadays" (108), when, in fact, he means Letitia herself. And "she tells you before the whole table how she was once on the verge of being head over heels in love with you and you wouldn't give her a tumble" (108). In other words, if he had dated her that summer and had become involved, she would have been thrilled. He has wondered how to earn that beautiful look, and all he had to do was act. Now that she has given him the answer in the form of nostalgic humor, he is bitter. "What it shows . . .," he says, "is how old she is getting to be" (108). The ironic burden of the story comes to rest squarely on him: what it shows is what a fool he has been.

The story of Miss Lenora Logan begins with a sense of alienation as strong as the one at the end of "The Other Times." The first-person narrator of "Miss Lenora When Last Seen" explains that Miss Lenora is "a missing person" (502) from Thomasville (virtually the same place as Thornton, which is based on Taylor's birthplace of Trenton, Tennessee). She has left town on hearing that her family home has been condemned to make way for the new high school, and it appears at first that her sudden automobile trip is an act of defiance. As the story develops, however, we realize that her departure is a retreat.

The first information about Miss Lenora concerns her strength of will. Her driving a car seems to be an expression of resistance: she "hates to be overtaken and passed" and she refuses to dim her lights first (503). She has also refused to sell her home to the county for a good price. After section 1 of the story reviews recent events, section 2 offers flashbacks in the form of four "occasions," in order to give a sense of her place in local history.

The narrator, an innkeeper who is one of her four favorite students from the past twenty-five years, explains her relationship to her students.

> She was eternally instructing us. If only once she had let up on the instruction, we might have learned something—or I might have. I used to watch her for a sign—any sign—of her caring about what we thought of her. . . .
>
> I suppose that what we wanted to know beyond any doubt, was that the old lady had suffered for being just what she was—for being

> born with her cold, rigid, intellectual nature, and for being born to represent something that had never taken root in Thomasville and that would surely die with her. (521–22)

According to an old truism that describes poor teaching, she teaches the subject, not the students. She loves knowledge, culture, and her vision of what Thomasville ought to be, but she does not love what it is. Her students want to know what she has "suffered" for being the way she is, because followers naturally desire compassion from their leader. If they are going to suffer the strain of learning, they want to know how their teacher has suffered and to know that she will suffer with them—they want compassion. But compassion requires one to be warm and responsive; she is cold and rigid. Since these words are uttered by one of her pets, Miss Lenora becomes less attractive.

For lack of warmth she has failed to move her students. Even her favorites have not turned out according to her wishes, and they do not "really know her" any better than anyone else (509) knows her. She keeps her distance by playing roles, never opening up and running the risks of being involved and hurt.

Often, as in "The Other Times," Taylor employs a narrator who is too blind or weak to see how he can alleviate the problem he describes. But the innkeeper does not deserve such suspicion. Although he does envy Miss Lenora's colorful nature, and he is too timid to do rash things, at least he discharges his responsibility to her by facing her with the bad news. The Logan family has always been haughty. What they have considered a proper concern for maintaining the quality of life in Thomasville has seemed to the townspeople a stubborn effort "to impede the growth and progress of our town" (507). Miss Lenora has inherited her family's arrogance.

She has preserved her dignity by playing the roles of traveler and teacher. Her trips have provided escape because they give her a chance to play a new role. Since her retirement from teaching, she has dressed for her trips in "outmoded finery" or dungarees (527), playing a role of one extreme or the other and stopping only at tourist homes where she can get to know those who own them. Then, playing elegant or folksy, she tells these people her life story in the third person: "For years, her only satisfaction in life has been her periodic escapes into a reality that is scattered in bits and pieces along the highways and back roads" (529–30).

The role of teacher is the last one we see her play in the story. When the narrator brings news of her defeat in court, she invites him in. He is fifty years old, but her manner shows that he is still the student, she the teacher. She even insists that their conversation is "like old times" (533), but the narrator knows it is not. She is facing a crushing defeat. The narrator remembers her from childhood as a beautiful woman with dazzling blond hair, and in old age with a "splendid white mane" with timeless "tortoise-shell combs" (530). Now she has cut her hair, put a blue rinse on it, and applied heavy makeup. She has become a stereotypical flighty old lady. Stronger evidence of the change is that she addresses him as "Dear boy" (530), which she would never have done before. At least in her old roles—teacher, society lady, folksy type—there was a certain vigor. Now she has surrendered all personality. At the beginning of the story and near the end, the innkeeper expresses his doubt that the people of Thomasville "will ever see her alive here again" (506). The ironic truth is that, whether she returns or not, the lady he knew is gone forever. Years before, a young Logan cousin at the school where Miss Lenora taught committed suicide from shame. Now Miss Lenora has been shamed, and she commits her own kind of suicide.

The self-discovery of Miss Lenora has been crushing. She did not really enjoy the trips—she calls them "dull and tedious" (505)—but they were a temporary escape from her home and her permanent, aloof identity. Now both are gone, and she is a nondescript, blue-haired, little old lady. She has never been ludicrous like Johnny and Annie Kincaid or Alfred and Louisa Dorset, but she has paid for her dignity. She admits to the narrator before her last trip: "I was unrealistic. I tried to be to you children what I thought you needed to have somebody be" (533). Having lost the brittle security of her family home, she is defeated and has traded her "cold, rigid, intellectual nature" for a bland exterior that anyone can accept, and maybe love.

In the stories in this chapter, time and decorum combine variously to reveal the characters. Sometimes they grasp the truth before it is too late (the writer in "1939" and *"Je Suis Perdu"*), sometimes after (Edmund Harper and Miss Lenora), and sometimes not at all (the Dorsets and the narrator of "The Other Times"). In each case, feeling their passage through time and seeing their place in their society make them consider who they are and what they ought to be. In these stories it is not only necessary but also good for people to discover themselves in terms of the world around them.

The Late Period—New Techniques, Old Concerns

Having published stories for forty years by the time *In the Miro District and Other Stories* appeared in 1977, Peter Taylor had created a solid set of expectations among his readers. As soon as they saw the byline of one of his stories in the *New Yorker* or the *Sewanee Review*, they anticipated elegant prose, a leisurely and digressive narrative, irony (sometimes comic, sometimes tragic), and characters either using or resisting decorum. Several pieces from *In the Miro District* fit that description. The title story and "The Captain's Son" are vintage Taylor, and are therefore included in a later section on the stories I consider his best in the late period. But his innovative verse stories turn from the norm dramatically.

Six of the seven stories examined here come from *In the Miro District*, and four of the six are in free verse: "The Instruction of a Mistress," "The Hand of Emmagene," "Three Heroines," and "Her Need." These all date from 1974 to 1976. The other two from this collection are much earlier in original publication: "The Throughway" (1964) and "Daphne's Lover" (1969). These two strike me as minor stories, as does the last one to be treated—"The Gift of the Prodigal" (1981), which is the only other story besides "The Old Forest" to be collected for the first time in *The Old Forest and Other Stories*.

The four story-poems above, "The Captain's Son," "In the Miro District," and The Old Forest," first appeared between 1974 and 1979. These seven stories, coming from an unusually rich creative period of five years, demand special attention. The last three embody the height of the expected in Taylor's work, but the other four represent an experiment by a man who has earned his reputation as an old-fashioned fiction writer. Of these, "The Hand of Emmagene" and "Her Need" are especially fine. Thus in this brief period from a career spanning half a century, Taylor devotees can find the best of the old and the best of the new.

The Late Period—New Techniques, Old Concerns

Why would the "acknowledged master of the short story in America," as some have called him, spend his talent on an experimental form so far into his career? An obvious answer would be that the good artist, thriving on challenge and invention, often decides to attempt new techniques once he has gone as far as he can with his traditional methods.

But there are deeper forces at work here than the mere need for challenge. As mentioned earlier, Taylor grew up, literally speaking, among poets (Tate, Ransom, Warren, Jarrell, Lowell), and his wife is a poet. Considering the company he has kept for all these years, a more natural question might be: What took him so long to get into poetry? He has also been drawn to the story genre because of his taste for compression, a technique that poetry takes a step farther than the short story does.

In a 1983 interview in *Contemporary Authors*, Taylor made some comments that provide a useful foreword to the readers of *In the Miro District*.

Taylor: Allen Tate was the person who really influenced me most, I suppose, and next John Crowe Ransom. Tate was simply my freshman English teacher, and at once he liked my writing, and he gave me the feeling that writing was important. And then he and I became great friends. . . . I studied with Ransom, too, for several years, and I think he had a real influence on the form my writing has taken. He made me write poetry and discouraged me from writing fiction. I think that made my fiction more compressed and made me turn to short stories more than to novels, because I did write poetry. . . . Other fellow students who became my lifelong friends were poets—Jarrell and Lowell. . . .

CA: Several of the pieces collected in *In the Miro District* are verse narratives. What led you to use that technique?

Taylor: I've always been interested in compression, trying to see how much one could put into a short story and yet have it as good as a longer story. In the end, short stories are not just short novels. They're much more intense, and the words have to do a lot more work. Just as in the lyric poem. . . . I'd tried for years before I printed these to write stories in formal verse with meter and rhyme, but that was always a failure. When my friends, like Lowell, began writing free verse, I began eyeing it and saying, "Well, why couldn't I do stories in sort of a relaxed way?" But I don't think they are poems. Lowell called them story poems, and he liked them, but I call them broken-line prose. I think the advantage is that you get two kinds of syntax and, most important, you get the line end. The form doesn't work unless the line end is significant, so that you're saying something by that word, the impact at the end of the line.

CA: . . . "The Captain's Son" is an old favorite of mine. . . .

Taylor: I had fun writing that story. I wrote it first in broken-line prose, but I couldn't sustain it. It's very hard. When those line ends cease to be functional . . . then I think, "Well I've failed." So I went back and put it all in regular prose. I also wrote the title story in that form originally.[46]

Both in their innovations and in their constancies, the stories in this chapter represent important features of the late period in Peter Taylor's short fiction.

"The Instruction of a Mistress" (1974)

The first story Taylor published in "broken-line prose," "The Instruction of a Mistress"[47] is different from any of his other short fiction in at least four important ways. First, although developing a story as the product of a journal or a letter dates back to eighteenth-century England, this is the only story he has produced using such a device. Second, juxtaposing things written by this man and woman, who were presumed to have been close, shows how little they understood each other and how alienated each of them was from all human warmth. Such blatant dramatic irony is rare in Taylor's work. Even as a young writer, he preferred subtlety. Third, this is his only story in which homosexuality and lesbianism appear. Fourth, though he sometimes uses unpleasant narrators in his stories, none are so repellent as the man and woman who speak from these pages. These differences make this story stand apart from the rest, and the narrative is so cold and cynical that it can finally repel the reader.

The arrogant poet writes of his mistress, "I was her college education" and then, in neat iambic trimeter, "And now, by God it's done" (39). He explains how he likes to take a dowdy girl and shape her into a woman to his specifications. "But that's the kind of girl I'm often /

Taken with, attracted to. I'm apt to like her / For all she's not but *could* be" (41). He will play Pygmalion, she Galatea. The mistress understands this when she works her way into his life by design, she and her lesbian lover, Maud, already knowing, "It's changing someone he likes" (47).

The irony grows as the mistress's posthumous letter reveals that she and Maud had schemed to get her into the poet's affections (insofar as he is capable of affection) and to discover the riddle of the "mysterious person" (46) whose death inspired his best poems. The mistress envies his literary stature and wants to discover the secret of his past power. She is something of a lesbian literary Delilah. A further turn in these twisted relationships occurs as the poet reveals in the third section something the mistress (now dead by suicide to ensure her fame) never guessed: that the mysterious beloved was a boy.

As the plot unfolds, some revealing parallels develop. The poet writes that she was "quick. / But she enjoyed nothing" (40). She writes of him, "He knows an immense amount about everything, including sex" (45). Both comments suggest that these people know much and feel little. They are cursed with intellectual pride and the insensitivity it causes. Further proof of this character flaw appears. She writes to Maud, "When it's you I'd love still / If I could love anyone but my-self—myself famous" (45). This is an elegantly turned poetic line like many in the story. He writes about the boy who kissed him and about the mistresses he has reared, "We must create creatures whom we can love. / Else I do not know what love is" (55). Despite the similarities in their natures—or perhaps because of them—these two could never have known each other, so great was their consuming pride. After both of them are established as utterly vile beings, the girl's suicide hardly matters.

The pattern goes on. We find at the end that he has started with a new girl whom he will make attractive, "Before she and I are through" (56).

In this story the alienation is absolute, the irony withering, and each character repellent. Though it appeared in the *New Republic*, it reads rather like a *New Yorker* story from the seventies—polished, ironic, frost-bitten with cynicism—and gives the false impression that the *New Yorker* has had more influence on Taylor than he has had on it.

In its combination of technique, subject matter, and theme, it is unlike any other story of Taylor's. In a negative way it is instructive, because it sets forth many post–Vietnam era clichés—blunt irony, homosexuality, lesbianism, suicide, cynicism, and nihilism—that Taylor has almost entirely avoided in the body of his short fiction.

"The Hand of Emmagene" (1975)

Being in verse form and containing the most grotesque violence Taylor has written, "The Hand of Emmagene" is, in obvious ways, another unusual story. Like "The Instruction of a Mistress," it stands alone. But beneath the striking differences of surface—the verse form, the portrayal of lust and violence—lies the most common thematic force in his work: decorum. Like his other stories, this one treats decorum on a serious level; there is not a superficial concern for manners, but a profound moral concern.

Emmagene is the most rural of Taylor's major characters. She is not quaintly country like Johnny and Annie Kincaid, who appear to be people of some modest means and position back home. Emmagene is the hard-working, lower-class daughter of a practical nurse. Like the Harpers in "Guests," the narrator and his wife have made a practice of helping country kin establish themselves in Nashville. He and his wife feel responsible even for promoting Emmagene's social life. As in "Guests," when the hosts cross the line between helping and manipulating, problems ensue. The decisive conflict of the story develops when Emmagene cannot meet their expectations without compromising herself.

Once again Taylor uses an unperceptive first-person narrator. Though he resembles Edmund Harper, he remembers little about his country origins. He and his wife, in their urban sophistication, have forgotten the mores of the common folk of Hortonsburg, where both they and Emmagene grew up. Considering their present comfortable life, they have never seen the world from her level. The narrator succinctly notes the "differences of style" (85), which are social and philosophical. She is a constant worker and a religious fundamentalist, and she is full of well-scrubbed, working-class virtue. The hosts inadvertently force Emmagene to a crisis because differences of style make open communication between hosts and guest impossible.

The narrator describes her hard work and extreme fundamentalism. In addition to cooking and cleaning without being asked to, she finds out that her hosts enjoy the fireplace in the evening and cuts wood and lays a fire daily. The narrator notes prophetically that she is skilled with an ax. In Nashville she travels to the far side of town to attend a suitable church, and back in Hortonsburg she and her family drove thirteen miles to church, "A church of a denomination that seemed always / To be changing its name by the addition of some qualifying adjective" (85). If Emmagene's origins haven't seemed laughable before, surely they do at this point. The narrator gives a telling detail. His comment on the church's name suggests that her church is not only fundamentalist but pentecostal, even primitive.

A dramatic illustration of her primitive side is her reaction to accidentally breaking a vase. Taylor begins his considerable emphasis on the importance of her hands, which are her most attractive feature and which, finally, symbolize her nature. She sometimes wanders the house, "Allowing her rather large but delicately made hands / To move lightly over every piece of furniture" (89) she passes. Here her hands reveal the passionate and potentially refined side of her, but when she breaks a vase, she reacts by "literally wringing her hands / As if she would wring them off, like chickens' necks if she could." She shows her primitive side as she wails, "I despise my hand for doing that. . . . I do wish I could punish it in some way" (90). The end is foreshadowed. Take one simple and sincere girl burdened by what will later be extreme guilt, with her hand again being the focus of her guilt, and add a fundamentalist's strictly literal reading of a figurative passage: ". . . if your hand causes you to sin, cut it off" (Matt. 5:30). The result is butchery.

As her hosts encourage her to have a social life, they don't realize that they are forcing her into a moral crisis. When Emmagene avoids dating the boys that have come from Hortonsburg because they are "trash" (92), she is not guilty of judgmental fundamentalism. She is telling the truth. She is also making a desperate effort to protect herself, because she knows any girl who dates one of these boys will be required to give sexual favors. No well-bred young men are available to her, a problem that her cousins can't grasp.

Whenever they try to help Emmagene improve her life—encouraging her to accept a ride from George, then to date him, and finally to wear a low-cut dress—her cousins force her deeper into conflict. The dress means nothing lewd to Cousin Nan, but to Emmagene—and to George—Emmagene's wearing it is a bold invitation. Finally with the dress, her inner turmoil bursts outward. On one side she loves the comfort and beauty of her cousins' home and feels obligated to them; on the other side she can't tolerate the evil that threatens her. She can either offend her hosts or sacrifice herself. She is trapped, and her painful compromise is to date George and masturbate him, feeling she is defiling her strong, beautiful hands in the process. Once she puts on the new dress, she knows George will not be satisfied with anything less than sexual intercourse. Emotionally torn, she physically dismembers herself.

A surprising feature of this story is that the sexual and violent forces are so restrained. Because the narrator gives so many details of Emmagene's appearance and behavior, we are much more involved with her inner conflict than with George's desire. Despite all of the sexual energy, this story is not lascivious. The most important conflict is within the well-scrubbed body and mind of Emmagene, and her presence fills the house with the smell of soap and of pies baking. Never does the perfume or musk of sex intrude.

By means of point of view and diction, Taylor introduces us to Emmagene at a condescending distance. Her backwardness and innocent severity even become irritating. Most readers can identify readily with her cousin but not with her. But as the story develops, she seems less peculiar and more sympathetic because the imagery counteracts the attitude expressed by the narrator. He shows us her beautiful hands that scrub, prepare food carefully, and fondle the furniture. What this severe girl lacks in social poise, she makes up for in energy and decency. By the end of the story we have seen enough of her suffering to feel compassion. Her death is not the pathetic end of a religious fanatic but the tragic loss of a moral person who finds herself under pressures too great to endure.

The compression of this story creates remarkable emotional intensity, and reading it is emotionally exhausting. To the extent that using broken lines may have helped Taylor compress his language, the verse form contributes to the effect of the story. Here, however, the lines and line ends don't seem nearly as important as in his other verse stories. The narrator's concern for and inability to understand Emmagene heighten the effects of imagery and action with a painful irony: the hosts who mean well inadvertently torment her. For Emmagene, decorum is an inscrutable curse.

"Three Heroines" (1975)

"Three Heroines," published in the same year as "The Hand of Emmagene" and written in the same form, is quite different. The energy of Emmagene's story comes from her physical activity and moral crisis, but the energy here pours from the irrepressible will of an eighty-six-year-old beauty. Taylor divulges facts about Emmagene at controlled intervals, but he presents the narrator's mother here with no apparent restraint. The methods of developing these characters are virtually opposite, but each character shows a strength of will that demands our interest and our respect.

Written in phrasal lines, which often have crucial words at the line ends, this piece reads more like a poem than a story. The action is even the stuff of lyric poetry: the old lady preparing for and attending her last big party. There is only enough narrative to generate the mood, and that narrative is sentimental, perhaps overwritten. But the woman herself is majestic enough to absorb the excess and not be obscured by it. Like a lyric poet Taylor turns the lady's "almost too silvery white mane" into a miniature portrait of her. He remembers,

> The old burnt-umber color, everything, how every hair
> And every strand once grew and fell, fell tenderly and
>   attentively
> Over a child that had mumps or measles
> And needed attention
> And no doubt once upon a time
> Over a lover, a husband.

(144)

This story shows the mother's last graceful flouting of death. As her allies in mortal combat she enlists her maid, Willie Mae, and Grandmother Haynes, whose example and words provide a model. Thus we have the three heroines of the title.

Grandmother Haynes, "Proud of all she had survived" (145), the woman who raked her diamonds from the ashes of her house burned by the Yankees, is the symbol of survival for his mother. And his mother serves a similar function for him—teaching him how to face death. Though Grandmother Haynes lived in Tennessee and her husband fought for the North, she "never surrendered . . . never betrayed either side" (152). Her secret is passed on to the narrator by his mother. "People said she was vain and frivolous. / She was most assuredly both—and capable and hardworking / And brave, too" (152).

The heroism that his mother displays is less dramatic: getting dressed for the party, telling of Grandmother Haynes all the while. When she puts her shoes onto her swollen feet,

> . . . swollen almost beyond recognition as feet. . . .
> One feels the pain in the room. In one's own feet.
> But my mother doesn't bat an eye. Not a wince from
>   her.
>
> (146)

Willie Mae's role is also significant:

> Mother stares up at me with eyes bright as a child's.
> The coloring of her rouge and lipstick seems real—
> More than real.
> As real as a doll's coloring.
> She is more real than life.
> She is something Willie Mae has put together.
>
> (147–48)

The thematic distinction made in this story is simple, but the mother's character is strong enough to give it resonance. The narrator mocks the doctor who has difficulty looking at his terminally ill mother at the party. He says the doctor knows nothing about death—which is a positive and significant human act. "He only knows about the cessation of life" (150)—which is a simple biological fact of no importance.

In this story, role-playing and decorum are indispensable means to living and dying with dignity. Following family precedent and the dictates of good breeding, the mother transfigures the pain of her dying body into a living celebration of her own life and of the lives before. Clearly Taylor tells us that one could do worse than to be "vain and frivolous—and brave" (154). As surely as decorum (or a failure to handle it) costs Emmagene her life, decorum enriches and prolongs the mother's life.

Peter Taylor appears to be much more interested in studying the truths and mysteries of human nature than in setting forth definitive statements of theme. His stories confirm his claim that he writes to discover and not to explain.

"Her Need" (1976)

Taylor wrote most of his early stories slanted through the feminine point of view (notably "A Spinster's Tale," "The Fancy Woman," and "A Long Fourth"). In the middle period however, he used a masculine point of view more often; in fact, of the eleven middle-period stories considered in this book, only "Bad Dreams" and "Two Ladies in Retirement" employ a feminine perspective. Though he presents women with sympathy and insight, in the middle and late periods, his most powerful stories are nearly always told in a masculine voice, "Two Ladies in Retirement" being perhaps the most significant exception. In "Her Need" he returns to a feminine third-person limited point of view as naturally as if he had just finished writing "The Fancy Woman."

In "Her Need," Peter Taylor, son of the Old South, depicts the plight of the modern divorcée as eloquently as any feminist could ask. So much for his social statement; his literary achievement is more impressive.

In one of the shortest stories he has written, his compression is so effective that the viewpoint character's insecurity, resentment, and rash action engross the reader. "Her girlhood gone" (133), along with her remarried husband, she holds onto as much of her former life as she can. When the bank that employs her repeatedly offers her a promotion (and a job location outside of the neighborhood where she grew up and married), she rejects it because of insecurity over the proposed change. She has already had one change too many with the divorce. Clinging to her familiar job and location, she seethes with resentment. To the professional praise that accompanies her last promotion offer, "suddenly she blurts out, / 'But why didn't you tell me twenty years ago I was a whizz?'" (135). Of course the banker didn't know her twenty years ago, when the only future she could imagine was marriage. Taylor elaborates on the sad and untimely twist of events: "For how could he have known her? / She didn't know herself then." She resents her naïveté and the society that exploited her. The woman's circumstances are plausible, and her embezzlement, prompted by frustration and anger, is an understandable, virtually tragic, conclusion to the story.

In this short narrative, the point of view quickly absorbs us, building character, conflict, and motivation to the bursting point within a few pages. Contributing to the emotional force of the story is a device Taylor mentioned in his 1983 interview—the impact of line ends. His ending words and his short lines infuse the narrative with poetic energy. The first line of the story establishes the conflict: "Her girlhood gone" (133). The alliteration carries into the second line, which develops the problem: "Her husband in the suburbs with this second wife." The line endings on the first page contain the essence of the story: "Gone . . . second wife . . . old part of town . . . reckless . . . to promote her . . . as a woman . . . until retirement." And later come these, which fill out the story with insistent echoes: "whizz . . . too late . . . alive . . . thoughtfully . . . transposing."

Taylor has taken a sad, though not uncommon, situation and used poetic intensity to turn it into a remarkably moving story.

"The Throughway" (1964)

After the poetic intensity and inner conflict of "Her Need," "The Throughway," in conventional prose, poses quite a contrast. Rather than a high pitch of conflict and anger, this story expresses a sullen dejection, an anger without heat or energy. The characters and tone of this story are unusual for Taylor's fiction.

Harry and Isabel, who have lived thirty-one years in the same house, have to leave because of the new throughway. At first we might expect heroic resistance and some thematic point about resisting urbanization and indiscriminate change, but Taylor avoids that cliché. Instead, these lower-middle-class, nondescript folks who have been considered "sane and sensible and unsuperficial people" (59) and who have been envied for their "stability," are unexpectedly disturbed. The throughway seems "to have undermined the very serenity for which Harry and Isabel were envied' (60), though we might have expected this threat to draw them closer together. Several of the Taylor hallmarks are missing here: no upper-class whites (or servant blacks), no subtle social interplay, no concern with decorum. If most of his stories can be said to give the effect of a color movie full of wood tones, pastel silks, and the greens and blues of opulent landscaping, this story is in black and white.

The third-person point of view is finally limited to Isabel's mind, so that her habitual optimism delays our discovery of Harry's true state. With all of the dialogue, the story sounds rather like a grim, naturalistic one-act play. In Isabel's perception Harry appears better than he is. The objective narrative at the beginning informs us that Isabel is "an excellent manager" (53) of their limited means. But she has lived fully, her bone china and wedding silver "used and enjoyed every day that came just the way he wanted her to" (63).

Further, the narrative explains: "It was her great pride that she could make something of nothing. And that was the trouble. She had made their nothing such a great plenty" (66). For her, living well has been the result of extending herself, of filling their house with her energy. For him, living well has been the product of contracting himself, of not having to strain at work or to take on new expenses at home. His being a handyman around the house is not a sign of initiative but an attempt to preserve the status quo.

Harry complains to Isabel, "I own nothing. . . . I made up my mind early in life to ask for nothing. I thought nothing was something they could never take away from me. But now it seems that isn't so. The world wants your nothing, even" (69). What he wanted was to be left alone in a comfortable daze, but everyone must face change. Even cautious Harry is not exempt. Until the coming of the throughway, Harry has managed time and place to his satisfaction. Now change disrupts both.

Later, Isabel disputes his creed of nothingness: "All along you've wanted *everything*, which is what everybody wants." (75). Here Isabel is presuming that Harry has felt the same natural desires she has, but she inaccurately transfers her outlook to him. On the day the moving van is to come, she is prepared, as always, to extend herself to the challenge, to be flexible. He has cancelled the van and accepts no changes; he is brittle.

Their admired stability has developed because two entirely different attitudes converged in a place that suited each of them for different reasons: she could make the best of what she had, and he had all he ever wanted. So long as they were static, their differences did not show or clash. Now, however, their differences appear irreconcilable. The throughway has opened a chasm between them.

"Daphne's Lover" (1969)

"Daphne's Lover" is back on familiar ground for Taylor—back to the broad streets, green lawns, and country club events of the Southern aristocracy. The characters hold our interest and offer surprises. But the first-person narrator here does have one problem reminiscent of Harry's. Harry lacks appetite, and though our speaker here has some appetite, he does lack the charm to fulfill his wishes. The narrator focuses the story on Frank Lacy, a tolerant and casual charmer and the narrator's best friend in high school. He sketches details from Frank's life in order to draw some conclusions about his own.

Frank differs greatly from the narrator. He lacks close family life and parental discipline, girls find him irresistible, and he handles their excesses with tolerance and grace. He is the narrator's alter ego, the loose, carelessly attractive romancer the speaker would like to be. The narrator, speaking from around age fifty, comfortably situated as a sedate college teacher, likes to think of "Frank off in Manhattan with his marriage and love affairs and work 'always in the vanguard of modern life,' as he puts it, and I with my not unhappy domesticity in a remote university town" (112).

When girls presume on him by expecting him to play a role for their amusement, he obliges in a tolerant manner. From the evidence at the beginning of the story, we might conclude from Frank's indifferent family atmosphere that he knows the pain of wanting expressions of love and not getting them; thus he obliges girls who display the needs that he has felt since childhood. Frank's responses to the girls' demands create several vivid, sometimes comic, images.

Janet Turner, whose mother is dead, is an especially pushy tomboy. In childhood her favorite stunt was to call Frank on the phone and tell him to save her. She would get the car started and headed down the street, then climb into the rumble seat with her bulldog and strike a helpless pose. Once Frank had jumped into the car and taken control, she would exclaim to the impassive dog: "Our hero saved us Clemson. How can we ever thank him?" (123). Forced into the role of matinee hero, he drives the car home without a word. In high school she continues to pester him, and he continues to react tolerantly, realizing that she can't help herself. When she throws his keys into the pool at night, disrupting his evening with his steady girlfriend, he merely comments, "Poor girl is not responsible" (119). Then with a breathtaking grace befitting John Barrymore or Ronald Coleman, he dives quietly from darkness into the lighted pool and retrieves the keys, making himself all the more romantic.

When another girl, earlier in high school, flirts with him shamelessly as she, Frank, and the narrator play ball, Frank sweeps her into his arms and gives her the kiss she has been demanding. Taylor portrays the scene like a slow-motion movie shot.

> It seemed the most natural thing in the world the way he took her
> in his arms, bending her backward over his right arm, with his right
> foot set forward a little, and kissed her directly on the lips. It seemed
> to me that they held the kiss for several minutes. Her left arm
> moved gently about his neck, and I won't ever forget how her free
> right arm fell loosely behind her as she bent backward and how re-
> laxed and beautiful and almost marble-like the arm seemed to
> me. . . . It was so like him to want to give her what she required of
> him. . . . She may have been the first girl he ever kissed. She may
> even—a year or so later, I would imagine—have been the first girl
> he ever took to bed. (129).

Meanwhile the narrator looks on helplessly, enviously.

Aside from these tableaux of Frank at his chivalrous best, one other
image is especially important—that of Daphne and Apollo as she turns
into a laurel to elude rape. The narrator admits that this scene, in its
various artistic renderings, fascinates him. His Limoges figurine of
Daphne and Apollo "is curiously relaxing" (125) to him because the
danger of romance never exists. She will always become a laurel before
his passion can be consummated. In real life, as Frank has proven repeatedly, the power of romance and of physical attraction demands to
be satisfied. The narrator has never known this power or taken the
risks that go with it. The title of the story refers not to Apollo but to
the narrator, who finds Daphne's permanently chaste condition a consoling idea.

Considering their friendship and their major differences in deport-
ment and effect on women, it is not surprising that the narrator lives
vicariously through Frank. Like Uncle Andrew in "A Friend and Protector," he lives on the excesses of another; but unlike Uncle Andrew,
the narrator neither causes Frank to be the way he is nor exploits him.
Frank has his real escapades; the narrator has a comfortable life, a suitable wife, and his images of Daphne.

The narrator admits that he needs "to participate more whole-heart-
edly in the lives of others" (130) now that he knows he is going to live
a stable life. Whereas Uncle Andrew enjoys Jesse's animal outbursts
and even supports them by making restitution afterward, the narrator
is merely an interested observer of Frank's adventures. He can't influence Frank's actions, and he certainly lacks the charm to emulate him.
All he can do is watch and live through him, just as millions do with
TV and movie stars.

Normally in such a story—and typically in a Taylor story—the author would treat the narrator ironically, revealing his fear but leaving him blind to his own ineffectual envy. The difference here is that the narrator does see the truth of his situation. Yet the process of the story presents us—and the narrator—with a mystery of human nature, leaving us with the unspoken question: Why do some people exude a magnetic attraction that others don't? The answer is: They just do.

Though the narrator expresses voyeuristic tendencies, he is harming no one, not even himself. He admits: "I tell myself that a healthy imagination is like a healthy appetite and must be fed. If you do not feed it on the lives of your friends, I maintain, then you are apt to feed it your own life, to live in your imagination rather than upon it" (130). Frank's burden is that his imagination and needs are so great that he has "fed" his life to them. By contrast, the narrator is not frustrated or resentful, only mildly dissatisfied and aware that people tend to have too much or too little of something, seldom just enough.

"The Gift of the Prodigal" (1981)

Starting out very directly in the present tense, the first-person narrator of "The Gift of the Prodigal"[48] describes the approach of his twenty-nine-year-old wayward son up his driveway, "coming to me *for* something, or *because of* something" (13). The men are a study in contrast: the son—young, in a suit and an unbuttoned shirt like a gigolo, healthy, full of life, often in romantic complications, irresponsible, always broke; the father—old, inclined to wear suits and ties, aching from bursitis, widowed, responsible, wealthy. More than anything else, the story is a character study, developing the simple irony that the prosperous father needs his son—troubles and all—more than the son needs him. But the point of the story seems to be that, as readers, we get to know the two men and contemplate the difference between superficial and fundamental human needs.

Most of the action of the story takes place in the father's mind as Ricky walks across the driveway, and it becomes apparent that the father—like Uncle Jesse in "A Friend and Protector" and like the narrator of "Daphne's Lover"—enjoys hearing of his son's exploits. He takes a veiled pleasure in the youth and recklessness of his son's wenching, gambling, fighting, and shooting. Most of the father's narrative in this story, set in Farmington, Virginia, is about Ricky: "It's an ugly story, I warn you, as, indeed, nearly all of Ricky's stories are" (17).

The proud father, "being the timid sort" (18) that he is, fairly delights in rehearsing his son's exploits.

Vicarious escape is the gift to his father from this Prodigal Son. About this Absalom the father says, "I ought to have let him hang . . . by his own beautiful locks" (29). The real problem of the story is not Ricky's: in fact, we never learn what Ricky's problem is, only that it will require money and perhaps legal action, depending on how far he has gone this time. Ricky's problems change. The father's problem doesn't: ". . . the old speculation: How many days like this one, how many years like this one lay ahead for me? . . . I'd someday look back with pleasure on what would seem good old days, which was an indication itself that they hadn't somehow been good enough. . . . If the good old days were so damned good, why had I had to think always how good they would someday seem in retrospect? . . . It's not them or my life but *me* there's something wrong with!" (25).

The real gift of the story comes not from the father, or from his three married responsible daughters, but from the prodigal, who meets his father's need. Each needing the other keeps them both alive. The father confesses, "I am wild with anticipation" to hear Ricky's latest troubles. "I forget my pains" (29). The most significant gift of the story is the escape the son gives his father. He escapes, first by being needed to solve problems, second, by participating vicariously in his son's escapades. The story concludes, "I am listening gratefully to all he will tell me about himself, about any life that is not my own" (30).

The stories considered in this chapter vary widely in narrative techniques and subject matter. For a writer who has built his reputation on continuity through the decades, Taylor displays a striking range in the stories published from 1964 to 1981.

The Late Period— Major Stories

The stories in this section treat themes of time, betrayal, alienation, and decorum, like most of Taylor's fiction. Their distinctiveness comes from their approach, rather than from subject matter or thematic focus. Each of these narratives is a protracted attempt to organize experience and clarify a mystery. Because these stories probe through layers of time and entangled relationships, they have more intricate plots than most of the others. Moving away from his original preference for a neutral or feminine point of view, Taylor uses a first-person male narrator for each of these stories, which primarily concern male initiation experiences.

The narrators of "Dean of Men" and "The Captain's Son" are both ironically rendered, telling the reader things they do not know themselves. In sharp contrast, the narrators of "In the Miro District" and "The Old Forest" are perceptive and trustworthy, and they achieve balanced lives as a result of their experiences. These stories do not propose simple answers to complex questions. They are neither simplistic nor didactic; rather they are exploratory. Dealing with complicated problems, they expose the subtle forces that influence their characters. The major stories, even more than the others, say too much to be reduced to neat statements of theme. Instead of ending with a flash of light, they typically conclude with a glow, the cumulative illumination of several vivid and truthful scenes.

"Dean of Men" (1969)

"Dean of Men"[49] consists entirely of a father's address to his son Jack. The father, now a college president in the 1960s, presents the history of his own professional disappointments and those of his father and grandfather, in order to teach his long-haired son, who is contemplating marriage, some crucial lessons about the world. In deliberate fashion the father defends his role in the "establishment" to his son, who is entering manhood warned by the popular wisdom of his generation not to trust anyone over thirty. By the end of the story the father has reinforced that warning in spite of himself.

Since he mocks his son's appearance at the outset, the story begins in a sarcastic, uneasy tone. But he believes that his message is so important that it transcends the friction or distance that exists between them. "Perhaps it is a story about you and me—about men" (14). He tells three stories of betrayal, revealing the surprising similarities of crises faced by him, his father, and his grandfather. The narrator moves back through time, his own crisis coming first, and once the other stories are told, he returns to his own career to sum up what Jack should learn from this eerie pattern of betrayal. In each instance a lengthy sequence of actions ends in a betrayal that the victim would never have thought possible, and at breakfast the victim releases his anger and frustration in an uncharacteristic outburst at a wife or daughter, then spends the Sunday alone at his office. After the betrayal and outburst the course of the victim's life changes.

The chief difference is that the narrator's father and grandfather change their careers visibly; whereas the narrator, though he tries to make a minimum of changes, gets a divorce. The wounded pride and humiliation of the narrator's father and grandfather cause them to react in ways the narrator never considers. The presentation takes a circular form, since the narrator only tells of his outburst at his daughter, then tells his father's story, his grandfather's, and finally returns to rehearse the events that led up to his own crisis. The decisive irony of this story, however, is that the speaker does not see the crucial difference between his experience and the others he describes.

In order to simplify the sequence, I will start with the story of his grandfather, from 1910. The grandfather, a United States senator, had been persuaded by Lon Lucas to run for governor in order to prevent a scoundrel from winning the office. With the support of Lucas's group, the grandfather would have won easily, but once he was committed to the race, they abandoned him, backed his opponent, who won, and got another man elected as senator unopposed. The narrator tells us that after the grandfather realized what was happening, he "hurled a silver dollar at my grandmother, who was still seated at the breakfast table" (12). This event marked his change. The coin landed in the sugar bowl where, for spite, she would not allow anybody to touch it. Since families of that era did not admit to having fights, the narrator does not know the details of their argument, but he does conjecture with confidence, "He forgot that he was not among men and he hurled a piece of money at his wife as he would have at some man to whom he had lost a bet" (12). Withdrawing from humiliation, he "retired from public life to the bosom of his family, where, alas, I cannot say he was greatly loved" (15). He further "withdrew almost entirely from all male company" and to his family became "the coarse-tongued tyrant of their little world" (15).

In similar fashion in the winter of 1930, the narrator's father, the president of an insurance company, was deserted by his "old school friend" Lewis Barksdale, who had influenced several dubious investments before the father assumed this presidency. When the father called for Barksdale's support in explaining how and why the investments were made, he agreed to come meet with the board of directors. At this point the narrator became directly involved because he accompanied his father to the train station on three consecutive days to meet a man who never arrived. Again the betrayal, again the humiliation. The outburst did not come until months later in the summer, but as the father was facing mounting financial pressure, he could not resist taunting the narrator's sister Margaret one Sunday morning at breakfast. Anticipating a proposal of marriage to Margaret from a rich boy whom even he liked, her father said, "It's just as easy to love a rich one as a poor one, isn't it, Margaret?" (10). After which his wife said, "I would be ashamed of myself if I were you" (11). Margaret stopped seeing the boy, a proposal never came, and her life was substantially altered by one remark made in an anger that she did not cause and could not alleviate. Afterward her father resigned, returned to practicing law, and "his real life was all at home" (23). Unlike his grandfather, the narrator's father was kind and loving at home, but "the look would come in his eye," (24) welling up from his profound sense of failure and loss.

This same sort of betrayal by a friend in business is the initiating action of *A Summons to Memphis*, Taylor's 1986 Pulitzer Prize novel. In the novel there are two daughters instead of one, both having their social lives shattered and their chances for marriage damaged by their father's precipitous move from Nashville to Memphis. The ramifications of the betrayal, the move, and the effects on the family members are more extensive in the novel, but the same basic pattern operates in the 1986 novel as in the 1969 story.

The narrator's own story comes from 1950. His downfall occurred when colleagues, who had induced him to speak against the acting college president, did not defend him when retribution came. But he, determined to profit from the experience of his forebears, decided to cause no trouble and resign quietly. Meanwhile, as he was discussing his predicament with his wife at breakfast on Sunday morning, his daughter Susie interrupted over his objection and said, "Why don't you go up to the trustees . . . and tell them how the president of the college is being unfair to you?" (4). He shouted at her, and his wife—just as his mother had done—said "I would be ashamed of myself if I were you" (50), and like his father and grandfather before him, he stormed out and spent the day alone in his office. The similarities are clear, but more important to the statement of the story are the differences. The narrative is curiously broken so that the reader sees all of the after-effects first: the narrator's outburst, then his father's, then his grand-father's. The precipitating events come next: the grandfather's, the father's, and the narrator's own.

Taylor uses the broken narrative to conceal from the reader the dif-ferences between the narrator's case and the others, differences the narrator himself refuses to see. The pattern of betrayal and reaction is so striking that the reader is tempted to let the narrator claim his place in the procession of decent and deceived men, but he does not deserve to be there. First, the father and grandfather had no means of self-defense. They were completely victimized before they realized what had happened, and they had no recourse. In his case, the narrator did. True, he was betrayed, but he could have filed a formal protest to the president or to the board of trustees. He might still be ruined, but he did have legitimate means to resist, which is precisely why he shouted at Susie. This scene raises my second point about how the narrator is unlike his father and grandfather. Susie inadvertently exposed the nar-rator's moral weakness by stating the truth as a child sees it. The women in the other stories were merely victims of undirected rage; Susie was a deliberate target because she spoke an intolerable truth. The third point of difference concerns the narrator's career. He left quietly and gratefully accepted help from Morgan Heartwell, who could have come to his defense earlier and who later apparently suf-fered from a guilty conscience. With his support the narrator advanced to dean, then to college president. What he did would be like his fa-ther's going to Barksdale and begging for a job or his grandfather's running for office again and asking Lucas for support. The narrator offers his success as evidence to his son that he has done the right things. Of course he has sacrificed his first marriage, his writing, and

ultimately his integrity; but, he rationalizes, "One sacrifices something" and "A man must somehow go on living among men, Jack" (38).
Really? Not on these terms, Taylor suggests.

The evidence of the story shows that the narrator's father, despite
his cruel and disastrous remark to Margaret, was the only good man in
the bunch. He took his defeat with dignity, and aside from his remark
to Margaret, he was kind to his family. The look of longing the narrator
sometimes saw in his father's eyes was the price that an honorable man
had to pay quietly for living "among men." Instead of looking at his
family's history and becoming brave or wise from the lessons of the
past, the narrator has become a coward. In this chronicle of betrayal,
the ultimate Judas is the narrator, who betrays himself. The power of
this story lies in its subtle and thorough revelation of the moral blind-
ness of its narrator.

"The Captain's Son" (1976)

The influence of one generation on the next is important in "Dean of
Men," and it is no less so in "The Captain's Son."[50] The story is set in
Nashville in 1935, and the importance of locale is apparent from the
first sentence, which begins an explanation of the unofficial "exchange" that has passed between Nashville and Memphis for two centuries. A young man who faces disappointment or disgrace in one city
repairs to the other to make a new start, and an interesting effect of
this practice is the interweaving of first and last names between the
cities. Beginning as it does, the story calls immediate attention to the
roles of decorum and alienation.

The middle-age narrator tells a story from his high school and college
years about the first three years in the marriage of his sister Lila and
Tolliver Bryant Campbell. Tolliver's father, Captain Campbell, had
been indebted to Lila's grandfather, a governor of Tennessee, for his
captaincy in the Spanish War, but when election time came, he had
defaulted on his debt by not lending his support. Instead, he had
moved to Memphis and pursued his own interests. But, the narrator
explains, this story was told in his family with great amusement because "At our house we tended to laugh at anything that was far in the
past or far in the future" (6). Great is the laughter in her house when
Lila says that she has met Tolliver Campbell of Memphis. They soon
marry and at the invitation of her father, but to his surprise, the new
Mr. and Mrs. Campbell move in with her family.

The events of the next three years are odd to say the least, and when the Campbells move out, their association with her family is practically ended. In this story decorum is the dominant force because, under the rule of good manners and family duty, the smallest statements change the course of people's lives. Unlike the servile rendition of organizational decorum that the narrator of "Dean of Men" makes up to justify his actions, these people respond to powerful expectations. Beneath the surface cordiality of "The Captain's Son" run deadly currents of betrayal and alienation. As in "Dean of Men," Taylor uses an ironic and unperceptive narrator who reveals a crippling flaw in his family without seeing it himself.

At the simplest level, the narrator, called Brother within his family, raises suspicion about himself. He seems to be a pleasant enough fellow, starting in a light tone and explaining, somewhat mockingly, the social ebb and flow between Nashville and Memphis. His regional self-deprecation is engaging, his directness refreshing: "There is an exchange between the two cities of Nashville and Memphis which has been going on forever—for two centuries almost. (That's forever in Tennessee.) It's like this: A young man of good family out at Memphis, for whom something has gone wrong, will often take up residence in Nashville. And of course it works the other way around" (5). To all appearances we are in the company of a guide who is perceptive, wry, and candid. He continues to explain the marriage of his sister, but as he proceeds, his prejudices begin to show, even though he voices them with a chuckle and a wink that is supposed to free him from blame: "For that's the way people are out at Memphis. They tend to take themselves and everything relating to themselves and their families too seriously" (5).

Even though Brother holds a light tone, his arrogance is beginning to show. Beneath his criticism that Memphians take themselves too seriously is this Nashvillian's clear implication that Memphis residents are too provincial for anyone to take seriously. Twice he says "*out at* Memphis" emphasizing remoteness and an implied lack of urban cultivation. He goes one step further. "He was raised and educated out there but he was born on a cotton plantation fifty miles below Memphis—in Mississippi, which, as anybody in Nashville will tell you, is actually worse" (6). From bad to worse. Brother is not the jovial wag he would have us think; he is a snob. First he looks down on people who are not of his place, then he extends his jests to those who are not of his time: "At our house we tended to laugh at anything that was far

in the past or far in the future. We were more or less taught to. . . .
Simply to be what we were in Nashville, circa 1935, was enough" (6).
What sounds like good-natured laughter has become derisive, con-
temptuous. Maybe making light of the past is fashionable in their social
group, but in laughing at the past, the family is divorcing itself from
history and responsibility. Human actions, past and future, do have
consequences, and the present is merely a pinpoint of time in the vast
parade of related events. A Southern gentlemen in 1935 may or may
not choose to follow the old ways, but he does not mock history. What
Brother presents as evidence of pleasantness is proof of the supercilious
nature of his family. These opening remarks, viewed from the end of
the story, are ominous, and they hint at the collective selfishness that
causes Father, Mother, and Brother to desert Lila and Tolliver.

Tolliver, Brother soon explains, came to Nashville under the "exchange"; his disgrace is that his wealthy parents are unregenerate alcoholics and his hope being to make a better life for himself. Brother
notes two irritating things about Tolliver from the start. One is that he
has no job and is content to live on his "rents and royalties" (9), unaware of how his leisure embarrasses Brother's family, which tries not
to appear too well-off in light of the Depression. The other is that
Tolliver unexpectedly takes people up on offers that they make out of
courtesy and not sincerity, whether the offer be that of a Coke from
Brother or of a place to live from Father. Brother observes, "I have
never since seen a young man who so plainly felt the urgency to marry
not just a certain girl but that girl's whole family" (12). What he does
not realize is that his two complaints and that observation are related.
Tolliver, having grown up with a surfeit of money and a dearth of affection, is desperate for a home, for a family.

Unlike Lila's family, "Tolliver didn't ever clown" (11); he has only
the uneasy sincerity of someone who wants desperately to be loved,
and he assumes that offers of kindness are genuine. The family laughs
at the past, clowns, and keeps up (or *down*) appearances by not looking
too comfortable while their neighbors are struggling. They make passing offers, like a place to live or a Coke, and never mean any of them.
They believe they do not "merely conform to social conventions" but
act "always from the right instincts" (17). Later, when Tolliver will not
hold a job for appearance's sake and he and Lila subsequently become
alcoholics, Father and Mother refuse to discuss the problem with
Brother and try to screen the Campbells from public view. When it
becomes apparent that they are not going to recover and will disgrace

the family, Father deliberately misunderstands Tolliver's saying he is going to take a trip to Memphis and asks Tolliver if he is moving there. All Tolliver can do to save face is say that he is.

Brother's family is altogether superficial. They are not observing good manners out of regard for others but because they can follow social forms, never be sincere, and always be safe. When Father sees the opportunity to be rid of Tolliver with the turn of a phrase, he jumps at it. No matter that he is impotent, both he and Lila are alcoholics, and they obviously need the help of people who can love them. The comfort of superficial living is that one can always find a way to escape deep involvement and messy situations—the very substance of love.

The betrayal in "The Captain's Son" is complete. Father and Mother never even visit Memphis, so happy are they to stay clear of trouble. Lila does finally have a son, but considering how the sins of the fathers have been visited upon the children, that is not much cause for hope. After Lila and Tolliver left, Brother moved into the fraternity house at Vanderbilt and "never lived at home again," (35) and he has never married. Perhaps he has taken the lesson of his parents to the logical extreme and shunned love entirely. Hiding behind decorum is one obvious fault that Taylor reveals through his insensitive narrator, but the effects of superficial living are invisible to the speaker. He does not see how his family, and he to some extent, betrayed his sister. He does not see the sad alienation as he makes sarcastic jokes about how Lila and Tolliver live now. "And what a life the boy must have had growing up with them! . . . If their livers stand up under it, they may actually survive to a very old age" (35). The lack of compassion in this story is chilling, and the doom of two families is almost assured. Decorum has been perverted. Here it is not a means of expressing respect but a shield against involvement.

"In the Miro District"

The narrator of "In the Miro District"[51] is perceptive and honest and gets none of the ironic treatment that Taylor uses to discredit Brother in "The Captain's Son." He does not review the past because he wants to cause his audience to share his amazement, as Brother seems to, or to justify his conduct, as the narrator of "Dean of Men" attempts. Instead he tells the story as an honest inquiry, and questions, asked and implied, pervade the story. He is an adult now, but he still does not understand the strange forces that pushed him and Grandfather Manley together and pulled them apart. There is nothing glib or self-serving in this narrator, just an honest desire to know: "To me it seems natural that I should think about all of this whenever I am lying awake at night or when I'm behind the wheel of my car on some endless highway. The memory of it raises questions in my mind that there seem to be no answers to. . . . I find myself wondering why, in that quaint Tennessee world I grew up in, it was so well established that grandfathers and grandsons were to be paired off" (160–61).

The irony of his relationship with his grandfather is that his parents' pushing them together makes both uncomfortable, and their partnership becomes one of alienation, man and boy feeling coerced and uneasy. Like Brother's family, this narrator's parents take lightly the past and the future and assume that members of those generations belong together. Inadvertently the narrator shows that his parents avoid dealing with the past and the future by patronizing the old man and the boy. The breaking point comes when the boy demands to be treated as an individual, as his grandfather always has. The irony of the story applies not to either of them, but to the boy's parents and to the social ethos they represent. They "put a grandfather and a grandson in so false a position with each other that the boy and the old man would one day have to have it out between them" (159). Since the grandfather and his grandson reject stereotypical roles, the strength of their personalities makes a clash inevitable. The narrator says this confrontation "left me with complications of feeling that nothing else had ever done. For my grandfather, of course, whose story this is meant to be— more than mine—it did something considerably worse than leave him with complications of feeling" (160). With equal parts of respect and resentment, the narrator tells his story, trying to fathom why child and grandfather are so helplessly alienated when each needs the other's love.

This story is set in Nashville in 1925, when the narrator is eighteen and his grandfather is seventy-nine. As a Civil War veteran, Grandfather Manley is expected to play the part of the old Southern gentleman and oblige everyone with war stories, historical speculations, and witty commentary. He refuses. He is an independent soul, who insists on living on his family farm despite his children's urgent invitation to live with them in Acklen Park on the fashionable west side of Nashville. Grandfather Manley mocks their airs, "referring to the city itself as the Miro District (because he said only an antique Spanish name could do justice to the grandeur which Nashvillians claimed for themselves" (161). He also subtly teases the narrator as he gets older, resenting the boy's refusal to visit him on the farm. The country man and the city boy are what they are, and neither will budge. "We couldn't understand or care anything about each other. Something in each of us forbade it" (164). Most of the old men of Manley's generation have moved in with their children and become "absurd martinets" or "domesticated as any old woman," but he is "an exception to all of this" (166).

Having shown Manley retaining his identity, Taylor goes on to show the narrator establishing his own in a series of three "face-offs." At the beginning of the story the narrator alludes to having been discovered with a girl in the bedroom his grandfather uses, thus foreshadowing the final confrontation. Knowing where all of this conflict is leading, the reader can concentrate on what each incident reveals about the old generation and the new. Though the boy is apparently caught unaware each time, he is subconsciously challenging his grandfather, knowing that he is likely to be discovered. On each occasion the parents are gone, so dual opportunities arise: first, to get faint revenge on his self-absorbed parents and, second, to offend his grandfather.

The first face-off occurs when Grandfather Manley finds the boy and two schoolmates drunk. The boy manages to stand and feels a vague eagerness for "the kind of dressing-down which he had never given me and which if he could have given me right then might have made all the difference in the world in our future relation—and perhaps our lives" (172). The boy is demanding to be recognized, taken seriously, punished in some significant way. He wants to bridge the gap between them by exciting rage or anything intense and personal. Instead the old man remains calm, which draws a stream of taunts in the form of questions from the boy, questions through which he retells his grandfather's old story of escaping a lynch mob and hiding for days near Reelfoot Lake. This story is the truth Manley has insisted on telling rather than the flowery lies about the Civil War that people requested. Hearing how well the boy has learned the account, he responds with his "sardonic courtroom laugh," which conveys enough casual contempt to have destroyed the case of many an opposing lawyer; thus the grandfather wins this battle by finally sending the boy off to bed.

The second run-in occurs six weeks later and involves the boy and several of his friends being discovered in their beds with girls, a distinct escalation of vice. Manley's first response is to wake the boy by striking him with his cane. The narrator thinks: "At last he has struck me! . . .

At last we might begin to understand one another and make known our real feelings, each about the other" (187). But then Manley calmly, even cordially, helps the "Eighth Avenue" girls on their way, which reduces the boy's rebellion to a youthful indiscretion. He explains the important distinction that contemporary decorum makes between Eighth Avenue girls and Ward Belmont girls. "The girls we had with us were not the kind of girls such a boy as I would spend any time with nowadays. That is why this part of the story may be difficult for people of a later generation to understand. With one's real girl in those days a girl who attended Ward Belmont school . . . one might neck in the back seat of a car. . . . But it was one's own manliness that made one overcome one's impulse to possess her" (186). Ward Belmont was one of the most prestigious girls schools in the South. According to the old code such girls should never, even in marriage, be the objects of consuming sexual passion.

The crisis comes two months later when the boy is caught violating decorum and makes no apology. Manley finds the boy in the house with a nude Ward Belmont girl. Since her very manner (even when discovered nude in the wardrobe) shows her to be from a good family, and since the boy loves her, Manley has not interrupted another rowdy escapade but a consuming passion of the sort that is a threat to approved behavior. Having been in his grandfather's room and in his bed, the narrator has carried out the ultimate defiance. Manley has defied social pressure by living in the country, telling his grim Reelfoot Lake story instead of the expected Civil War stories, and refusing to participate in Confederate Decoration Day. He has rejected the mask of the charming old gentleman. He has been a genuine human being all of his life, as boy soldier, lawyer, and farmer, and he refuses to surrender his identity to placate his daughter and son-in-law. Ironically, he cannot face the boy's individuality.

The boy rejects the attitude of the old order toward sex, the belief that it was not something honorable men talked about or pursued vigorously with women of their own class. Grandfather Manley holds onto this outlook, even to the point that hearing his son-in-law discuss prostate surgery strikes him as "unseemly." Now, just as Manley has maintained his identity by flouting some expectations of conventional behavior, the boy establishes his identity by defying others. The problem is that his grandfather does not know what to do. Even though he has rejected the stereotypical role of the Confederate veteran, he has dealt with his grandson as a stereotype and not as a distinct human being. Thus when the boy does something unexpected and outside of his prescribed role, Grandfather Manley leaves the house without a word, goes home, and puts on a black serge suit, starched collar, and string tie, and never thereafter misses a Decoration Day celebration. He is too set in the ways of the old order to face the boy's misconduct and talk to him. Rather than berating him or trying to understand him, he withdraws, incapable of admitting to himself what his eyes have seen.

Until that final confrontation, Manley is closer to his grandson than to his own daughter. The similarities between grandfather and grandson have drawn them into an uneasy association, though their differences finally separate them. They do not like being forced together and being deprived of their own wills, but they are attracted to the staunch integrity of each other. Sadly, Manley's shock at the role of sex in the new order is so great that he retreats to the role of Confederate veteran, moves in with the boy's parents and fulfills their every wish; and man and boy end "a thousand years apart, or ten thousand" (199). In a spiritual sense, Manley dies at the third confrontation, and his appearances to the boy thereafter are those of a walking shadow. Ever so painfully, the narrator has used his grandfather to define himself. Though his generation and values differ from the boy's, he has sufficient identity to be a whetstone for the blade of youth. The shame is that he lacks the love necessary to carry on the relationship, intensify the conflict, and resolve it in love.

The consolation of "In the Miro District" is that a young man of passion and integrity emerges from the sham world that his grandfather has resisted for so long. The pity is that his grandfather cannot accept the boy as a distinct human being. In this story Taylor shows what a high price decorum can exact from people. He also shows that integrity can be enough to resist the obliteration of individual identity. People like the narrator and his girl represent the hope of the new order.

"The Old Forest" (1979)

An element of mystery influences the tone of many of Taylor's stories; however, in "The Old Forest"[52] an actual investigation is the main action. The obvious question for much of the story is: Where is Lee Ann Deehart? The deeper questions for the narrator are: What makes

Lee Ann and Caroline act as they do? and, Why are these women so different and yet so strong? "The Old Forest" deals with changes in social ethics as "In the Miro District" does; but in the earlier story the boy is the leading force for change. In the later one two young women of different social classes lead the way while Nat Ramsey, the narrator, follows. In both stories young characters act boldly to uphold their integrity, resisting decorum when they need to and conforming to it when they can. A major thematic step Taylor takes in "The Old Forest" is to use Lee Ann, who is of the same social class as the "Eighth Avenue girls," and Caroline, who is of the same social background as the Ward Belmont girl, as alternate approaches to living with the demands of decorum. Lee Ann disregards it, Caroline uses it to her advantage, and both girls function in their social strata without compromising their integrity.

The rise of the new order in Southern society is a dominant concern in Taylor's late period. The boy and girl from the Miro District, sincere, passionate eighteen-year-olds challenging the assumptions of their forefathers, represent the new order of 1925. "The Old Forest," set in Memphis in 1937, follows the progress of the new order into the next stage. World War I sealed the reunion of the South with the rest of the nation as it belatedly joined the twentieth century; but as Allen Tate noted, the South hesitated and looked back before entering the American mainstream.

The Jazz Age chronicled by Scott Fitzgerald blared in the North, but in the South an agrarian society still struggled with industrialization and urbanization, as Taylor's mentors Ransom, Tate, and Warren demonstrated in 1930 with their essays in *I'll Take My Stand*. Taylor never expresses the Agrarians' suspicion of city life, but urban and rural values do come into conflict in his stories, as with the country Grandfather Manley and the city boy. When man and boy face each other in the hallway of the Acklen Park house, the nineteenth-century South and the twentieth-century South confront each other. "In the Miro District" shows social forces in the aftermath of World War I, and "The Old Forest" examines the condition of the new order on the eve of World War II. Taylor takes great care in presenting the nuances of that vanished social order, mindful that Memphis in 1937 is a society as foreign to the modern reader as Flaubert's France or Fielding's England. The reader does not know exactly how much time has elapsed between the events of "In the Miro District" and the telling of the story, but the action of "The Old Forest" occurs "forty years ago and a little more" (31). The narrator is clearly concerned about how the events of the story appear in light of American social history circa 1979.

The precipitating problem of the story is an automobile accident. Nat Ramsey's car is hit by a truck sliding out of control on an icy road in Overton Park, and his "female companion," Lee Ann Deehart, jumps from the car and disappears into the woods. This minor collision occurs a week before he is to marry Caroline Braxley, and Lee Ann's disappearance nearly puts an end to the wedding plans. In the subsequent action Nat becomes an investigator and observer, reporting the actions of the women. He explains, "It was not unusual in those days . . . for a well-brought-up young man like me to keep up his acquaintance, until the very eve of his wedding, with some member of what we facetiously and somewhat arrogantly referred to as the Memphis demimonde. (That was merely to say with a girl who was not in the Memphis debutante set)" (31). In short, he is not guilty of misconduct, only caught in an awkward situation.

The charm of working girls like Lee Ann is that they are independent, high-spirited, usually intelligent, and altogether unrestricted by the rules that restrain the debutantes. He admits that such a dual social life must seem false to "the liberated young people of today" (33). (Ironically, Lee Ann and her peers are the forerunners of the "liberated" later generations.) He admits that the wreck, disappearance of Lee Ann, and the temporary disruption of his wedding plans are minor events in the course of an adult life in which he has served in World War II and suffered painful losses: both of his brothers died in the Korean War, his parents in a fire, and two of his children in an accident. But he recalls this incident because it happened before the cataclysmic changes of the modern world and it shows that "life *was* different in those times. . . . Our tranquil, upper-middle-class world of 1937 did not have the rest of the world crowding in on it so much. . . . The contrasts . . . seemed quiet and well ordered and unchanging" (42–43).

When Lee Ann runs from the car into the Old Forest of the park—a flight into the forest primeval, an undisturbed primitive area in the midst of the city, a symbol of natural freedom in the midst of a regimented society—she initiates her conflict with Caroline. She flees in order to be free of scandal, and she stays in hiding when Nat searches for her because she owes him nothing and, finally, does not want her own private life and the identity of her grandmother exposed to publicity. Caroline, hearing Nat's report, tells him that he will have to find

Lee Ann and that it won't be easy. Without proof that Lee Ann is safe and not pregnant, Caroline knows that her marriage is in peril and she will have to call it off.

What develops, then, is a "struggle of women for power among themselves" (49). Lee Ann's power lies in her lack of social ties, Caroline's in her social status and her ability to manage her fate within a prescribed code of behavior. From the outset Lee Ann is a more romantic and more naturally appealing character to the reader, an effect that Taylor achieves deliberately. The dramatic challenge of the story, however, is to take one of society's "spoiled rich girls" and make her even more attractive to the reader. Taylor commented in a 1987 interview,

> I recognize that writing about the so-called high society and making it appealing to my readers is a challenge. In "The Old Forest" I deliberately made the heroine a society girl, a debutante. . . . But I said to myself, it would be more interesting to see if I can make this society girl appealing as a human being. . . . I wanted to see human beings set in certain historical situations from which they can't escape. . . . The only power that she had was to be a rich married woman in Memphis, and that was all that was offered to her.[53]

Nat explains that such girls "considered themselves the heirs to something, though most likely they could not have said what" (49). He observes that we are all heirs to something, and "even the sad generation of the sixties and seventies—is heir to more than it thinks it is, in the matter of manners" (50). The rebels of the sixties and seventies rejected all traditions and claimed complete freedom. Nat knows they were deluded and that nobody is utterly free of social forms and influences. Caroline, however, takes decorum as an ally, assumes the initiative, and finally leads Nat to Lee Ann. She is heir to a place in the world that suits her. She loves Nat, is pleased with the prospect of being his wife and taking a position of authority in the world in which they have grown up. The delicate point is that they can proceed with their marriage only if Lee Ann is found.

In Nat's search he does not find Lee Ann, but his conversations with other girls of the demimonde reveal more about Lee Ann's world, making the mysteriously missing girl even more attractive. (The narrative does not swing the reader's sympathy decisively toward Caroline till the end of the story.) Nat, from a world of distinctions and traditions, comments that these girls, regardless of parentage or money, make "no distinction among themselves. . . . They would have been highly approved of by the present generation of young people" (58). Rather than taking *demimonde* literally as "little world," one might do better to think of it as the *nouveau monde*, the "new world"; for that is certainly what Lee Ann and the rest represent. They are the embodied foreshadowing of the liberated youth of the Vietnam era. They are "bookish and artistic," and he admires the girls he questions for the "boldness" with which they keep up the deception to shield Lee Ann, for their "personal, feminine beauty" (59), and even for their vulnerability. Their only resources are their individual wills and their collective loyalty, since they have no social institutions to guide or protect them during a crisis.

A subtle and encompassing irony in this story lies in the ultimate power that the old order exhibits. In his search, Nat confers with his father and several other community leaders, among them lawyers and ministers, and he notes their "feelings of responsibility for such girls" (66), which seem unwarranted because these girls want no help. Nonetheless, these are "a generation of American men who were perhaps the last to grow up in a world where women were absolutely subjected and under the absolute protection of men. . . . They spoke as if these were daughters of dead brothers of their own. . . . And so these men of position and power had to act as surrogate fathers during a transitional period" (67). Their attitude is reminiscent of Grandfather Manley's in "In the Miro District" when he helps the girls find their things and leave the house, speaking to them "gently and without contempt or even condescension" (188). In that story the old order is defeated when the old man cannot face who his grandson is, but in this story these fathers show a paternal control and Caroline, heroine of the old style, prevails.

On the surface level of the story, the mystery is solved when Caroline finds Lee Ann, makes sure she is unharmed, and secures Nat's promise never to see her again. But while Caroline is inside the house resolving all doubts and securing the future, Nat sits in the car, reviewing his feelings from the past four days, and realizes that "Lee Ann Deehart had come to represent feelings of mine that I didn't try to comprehend. . . . I felt that this was my last moment to reach out and understand something of the world that was other than my own narrow circumstances" (79–80).

As the whole story suggests, Lee Ann appeals to Nat more for what she represents than for who she is. She embodies freedom, risk, the unexpected. Dating her and taking a Latin class purely because it appeals to him are expressions of yearning from this proper young man who has graduated from college and begun a career in his father's cotton business. Lee Ann represents the rebellious side of his nature, while Caroline represents the responsible side. She confesses to Nat her "jealousy and resentment of the girl—of *that* girl and of all those other girls" (85) who are free to move on the fringes of Memphis society and poach boyfriends and seduce husbands while the women like Caroline have no choice but to defend their ground. They have none of the choices available in the demimonde. What disturbs her, says Caroline, is Lee Ann's "freedom to jump out of your car, her freedom *from* you, her freedom to run off into the woods" (85). Puzzled, Nat asks, "*You* would like to be able to do that?" to which she says, "*Anybody* would, wouldn't they? . . . *Men* have always been able to do it" (85). Such girls are free and appealing because "they have made their break with the past" (85), but Caroline, having a well-defined place in the world, has no choice. She finally explains to Nat, "Power, or strength, is what everybody must have some of if he—if she—is to survive in any kind of world. I have to protect and use whatever strength I have" (88).

Caroline's victory over Lee Ann, then, might be interpreted symbolically as Nat's surrender of his free spirit to his conformist urges. Such a conclusion, however, does not take into account the last paragraph of the story. Nat states that he later decides to leave his business, spend years in graduate school, and become a college teacher—all of which upsets Caroline's social order substantially. But she knows how precious security and freedom are, and wishes them as much for him as for herself: "She would dedicate her pride of power to the power of freedom I sought" (89). Here the old order has won by virtue of strength of character and willingness to change. Taylor is not wedded to tradition or to change. The importance of his characters' actions is not that they are conservative or liberal, but that the characters are honest with others and true to themselves.

Conclusion

Victorian-realist strikes me as a legitimate label for Peter Taylor. Like all labels, it oversimplifies, but it does emphasize his place in the large expanse of fiction of manners, and it applies both to his characterization and his plot development. He stresses the role of decorum in the lives of his characters, while he sketches them in measured realistic detail. The Victorian plot tends to be large and intricate, while the realistic plot shows more economy of action and less artifice. Taylor's narratives frequently exhibit digression, yet he tells us, "Compression is everything."[54] He insists on having the benefits of both economy and prodigality in his stories. He is a comfortably modern man in the themes of his stories; he accepts the present world as it is, though he does not like all he sees. Still, he will not lock up the attic and deny the past.

The fiction of Peter Taylor is a delicate balancing act of techniques and themes. Digressions fill his most powerful stories, but every time he takes us off the straight path of the narrative and into the woods, we return with a richer sense of the countryside and discover that we are much farther down the trail. So his digressions do break the immediate progress of a narrative, but they compensate us with depth. "The fact that Peter Taylor's best stories are like miniature novels has been noted before. His narrative method is to hover over the action, to digress from it, to explore byways and relationships, to speculate on alternative possibilities—in short, to defy the conventions of brevity and concentration that we usually associate with the genre."[55] By stretching the limits of a story toward the richness of a novel, he balances his art between the two. In Poe's spirit of the short story, he holds onto a length that can be read "in one sitting" (though sometimes a long sitting), but he does not confine himself so strictly to "unity of effect." In that way he is like a novelist. The tension between digression and compression generates a Renaissance *copia*, making us feel that the story's cup is on the verge of overflowing. The tension creates the dynamic energy of expectation.

Similarly, he sees the inseparable virtues and vices of decorum. He readily acknowledges the folly (even puts it in the title of a story) of living in the past, but exposes the comparable error of those who presume to forget history. For modern man to be a whole creature, not a fragmented, confused, and self-destructive one, he must embrace decorum and innovation with tentative arms. Of course, Taylor's characters who deal with change err in one direction or the other: bracing themselves against the doorway from the past, or flinging back the door and racing into the future heedless of what they leave behind.

The trick of Taylor's narratives is to deliver potent passages and scenes in an apparently casual fashion. With the forward and backward motions, his action and reiteration appear strewn across the pages. From a reflective distance, however, the pieces of his stories are no more random than the pieces of a carefully designed quilt. Partially because of his upbringing and disposition and partially because of premeditation, he stitches charming, sometimes intricate, quilts that feel good to the touch but only reveal their design at a distance.

Having stressed Taylor's uniqueness, I will follow a reverse pattern, exiting this section as I entered, returning now to influences. James and Chekhov are the consensus favorites as major influences. James, for his psychological depth, and Chekhov, for his sharp and revealing surface details, both deserve mention. But giving them too much credit is a mistake we are inclined to make if we listen to Taylor's comments selectively, hearing what we expect to hear. He also mentions Tolstoy and Lawrence on occasion. They seem to have had as much effect as the others.

Tolstoy at his best flashes the perfectly revealing glance of Chekhov and follows through with the depth of nuance of James. Tolstoy also employs a disarmingly frank and warm narrative voice, and he immerses us in his fictional world. Taylor's narrators—whether first or third person and whether perceptive or unperceptive of subtle points—tend to be intelligent, convivial people. Thus while we listen to them and try to decide what to make of them and of their stories, we have usually spent our uncertain moments in pleasant company. Even when the news in Taylor's stories is bad, the company is usually good. This warmth resembles the feeling that Tolstoy often generates.

Speaking of feeling, Lawrence deserves mention. Peter Taylor commented in an interview with Stephen Goodwin that he enjoys the texture and prose rhythms of Lawrence's short stories. In our era Taylor is as good a candidate for the master of rhythmical prose as John

Updike. One from the South, one from the North, both thoroughly lyrical—they carry on today in the tradition to which Lawrence contributed.

Doubtless, the above influences, as well as those of Taylor's fellow Southern writers, have been significant; nevertheless, I believe the most decisive influence took hold of Peter Taylor years before he read the nineteenth-century greats or met their twentieth-century successors. He dedicated his *Collected Stories* to his mother, giving her credit for many of the stories contained therein. More important than the stories, she gave him her method. She is surely more the source of his rhythm than Lawrence ever could be, even though reading Lawrence may have awakened him to the possibilities of rhythm. The first voice we hear in this world naturally has a profound effect. And if that first voice happens to tell stories often, the effect on a writer cannot be less than powerful. Along with the rhythm of his mother's voice Taylor also seems to have picked up her point of view. Critics have often noted the predominance of feminine points of view in his early period. Taylor seems to have been listening to a voice from childhood in most of his stories from the thirties and forties.

Along with his mother he listened to other storytellers, and the experience gave him more than craft. It gave him wisdom. He said in 1981,

> My theory is that you listen to people talk when you're a child—a Southerner does especially—and they tell stories and stories and stories, and you feel those stories must mean something. So really writing becomes an effort to find out what these stories mean in the beginning, and then you want to find out what all stories you hear or think of mean. The story you write is interpretation. People tell the same stories over and over, with the same vocabulary and the same important points, and I don't think it ever crosses their minds what they mean. But they do mean something, and I'm sure that is what influenced me. . . .
>
> I like to think that I write in response to my experience, to discover what I think and what I experience, because I think that's what writing is; a discovery of what you know and a discovery of what you think.[56]

Getting into his first Peter Taylor story, a reader might ask where this leisurely, rambling speaker is taking him. The characters are solid and their problems matter, but where is the urgency that a short story is supposed to have? Where is the forward-leaning momentum? There is momentum, but it is diminished and masked by digressions. The momentum is not overt but cumulative.

We seldom grasp profound insights in a single glimpse; rather, we see reflections of light from an underlying truth. As the archaeologist must unearth several pieces of an old community before he sees its pattern, so must the student of human behavior. Even when he has exposed a clear pattern of foundations and artifacts, the wise explorer is never so brash as to assume he has explained the whole mystery of why people lived as they did.

By the same token, Peter Taylor is an archaeologist of human mysteries, not a grave robber. He does not dig hastily, wrench out a few dazzling observations, and call it a day. He probes the same ground repeatedly, patiently, even reverently, and leaves us with a depth of mystery, along with moments of clear vision, suggesting that more always waits beneath the surface.

Notes

1. Richard Howard, "Twenty-one Holding Actions by a Modest American Master," *New York Times Book Review*, 19 October 1969, 4 and 26; William H. Gass, "Look at Me . . . ," 5 and 44.

2. Howard, "Holding Actions," 4.

3. Joyce Carol Oates, "Realism of Distance, Realism of Immediacy," *Southern Review* 7 (Winter 1971):301.

4. Roger Sale, "Its Discontent," *Hudson Review* 22 (Winter 1970):710.

5. Barbara Raskin, "Southern-Fried," *New Republic*, 18 October 1969, 29.

6. Jonathan Yardley, "Taylor's South," *New Republic*, 22 November 1969, 27.

7. Anatole Broyard, review of *In the Miro District and Other Stories*, *New York Times Book Review*, 3 April 1977, 4.

8. Keith Opdahl, "His Stories Lay Quiet Siege," *Christian Science Monitor*, 22 January 1970, 11.

9. John Thompson, "The Clever, the True, and the Marvelous," *Harper's*, November 1969, 134.

10. Allen Tate, "Peter Taylor," *Shenandoah* 28 (Winter 1977):10.

11. "The Furnishings of a House," *Kenyon Review* 1 (Summer 1939):308.

12. *The Collected Stories of Peter Taylor* (New York: Farrar, Straus and Giroux, 1969).

13. Flannery O'Connor, "The Fiction Writer in His Country," in *Mystery and Manners* (New York: Farrar, Straus and Giroux, 1961), 34.

14. O'Connor, "Some Aspects of the Grotesque in Southern Fiction," in *Mystery*, 44.

15. Robert Penn Warren, introduction to *A Long Fourth and Other Stories* (New York: Harcourt, 1948), viii.

16. Warren, introduction to *A Long Fourth*, ix.

17. Thomas Daniel Young, "The Contemporary Scene," in *Tennessee Writers* (Knoxville: University of Tennessee Press, 1981), 92.

18. Stephen Goodwin, "Life Studies," *Shenandoah* 21 (Winter 1970):102.

19. William Peden, "A Hard and Admirable Toughness," *Hollins Critic* 7 (February 1970):3.

20. Peden, "Toughness," 7.

21. Young, "Contemporary," 92.

22. Walter Clemons, "Southern Comfort," *Newsweek*, 11 March 1985, 74.

23. Richard Eder, review of *The Old Forest and Other Stories*, *Los Angeles Times Book Review*, 3 February 1985, 1.

24. Jonathan Brumbach, *Moderns and Contemporaries: Nine Masters of the Short Story* (New York: Random House, 1968), 344.

25. Herschel Gower, "The Nashville Stories," *Shenandoah* 28 (Winter 1977):43.

26. Albert J. Griffith, preface to *Peter Taylor* (Boston: Twayne, 1970), no page number.

27. Robert Towers, "A Master of the Miniature Novel," *New York Times Book Review*, 17 February 1985, 26.

28. Griffith, preface to *Taylor*, 153–54.

29. Walter Sullivan, "The Continuing Renaissance: Southern Fiction in the Fifties," in *South: Modern Southern Literature in Its Cultural Setting*, eds. Louis O. Rubin and Robert D. Jacobs (Garden City, N.Y.: Doubleday, 1961), 28.

30. Walter Sullivan, "In Time of the Breaking of the Nations: The Decline of Southern Fiction," in *Death by Melancholy: Essays on Modern Southern Literature* (Baton Rouge: Louisiana State University Press, 1972), 89.

31. Quoted from *Collected Stories*. Hereafter, references to "A Spinster's Tale" will be cited in the text.

32. Stephen Goodwin, "An Interview with Peter Taylor," *Shenandoah* 24 (Winter 1973):8.

33. Quoted from *Collected Stories*. Hereafter, references to "The Fancy Woman" will be cited in the text.

34. Goodwin, "Interview," 8.

35. Quoted from *The Old Forest and Other Stories* (Garden City, N.Y.: Dial Press, 1985). Hereafter, references to "The Scoutmaster" will be cited in the text.

36. Quoted from *The Old Forest*. Hereafter, references to "A Long Fourth" will be cited in the text.

37. Quoted from *Collected Stories*. Hereafter, references to "Cookie" will be cited in the text.

38. Quoted from *Collected Stories*. Hereafter, references to "What You Hear From 'Em" will be cited in the text.

39. Quoted from *The Old Forest and Other Stories*. Hereafter, references to "Bad Dreams" will be cited in the text.

40. Quoted from *The Old Forest*. Hereafter, references to "Two Ladies in Retirement" will be cited in the text.

41. Quoted from *The Old Forest*. Hereafter, references to "A Friend and Protector" will be cited in the text.

42. "1939" and "*Je Suis Perdu*" are quoted from *Collected Stories*. Hereafter, references to both stories will be cited in the text.

43. Ian Hamilton, *Robert Lowell: A Biography* (New York: Random House, 1982), 221.

44. "Guests" and "Venus, Cupid, Folly and Time" are quoted from *Collected Stories*. Hereafter, references to both stories will be cited in the text.

45. "The Other Times" and "Miss Lenora When Last Seen" are quoted from *Collected Stories*. Hereafter, references to both stories will be cited in the text.

46. Ann Evory and Linda Metzger, eds., "Taylor, Peter (Hillsman)," in *Contemporary Authors*, New Revision Series, volume 9 (Detroit: Gale, 1983):498–90.

47. "The Instruction of a Mistress," "The Hand of Emmagene," "Three Heroines," "Her Need," "The Throughway," and "Daphne's Lover" are all quoted from *In the Miro District and Other Stories* (New York: Farrar, Straus and Giroux, 1977). Hereafter, references to these stories will be cited in the text.

48. Quoted from *The Old Forest*. Hereafter, references to "The Gift of the Prodigal" will be cited in the text.

49. Quoted from *Collected Stories*. Hereafter, references to "Dean of Men" will be cited in the text.

50. Quoted from *In the Miro District*. Hereafter, references to "The Captain's Son" will be cited in the text.

51. Quoted from *In the Miro District*. Hereafter, references to "In the Miro District" will be cited in the text.

52. Quoted from *The Old Forest*. Hereafter, references to "The Old Forest" will be cited in the text.

53. W. Hampton Sides, "Peter Taylor," *Memphis*, February 1987, 117.

54. Caryn James, "Symbols and Themes Mature into Plots," *New York Times Book Review*, 17 February 1985, 26.

55. Towers, "The Miniature Novel," 26.

56. Interviewed by Jean W. Ross, "Peter Taylor," *Contemporary Authors: New Revision Series*, volume 9 (Detroit: Gale, 1983), 489.

Part 2

THE WRITER

Introduction

Beneath the surface of Peter Taylor's stories, the reader can sense an ironic, nostalgic author. Perhaps, like any Southern gentleman, he reveals himself as much by what he does not say as by what he does. He avoids excess and is wary of anyone who is loud, vulgar, or ostentatious. When his characters occasionally show these vices, he presents them with detachment. He is too much the writer to judge them outright and too much the gentleman to indulge them.

The selections that follow provide insight into this modest man. Personal reminiscences and interviews illuminate a craftsman whose first concern is not art but people. These pieces come from his teachers, fellow writers, friends, and a former student.

Two Peters:
Memory and Opinion

*Robert Penn Warren**

There are two Peter Taylors for me—perhaps more, but two for this moment. To begin with one. There is the tall, somewhat lanky man (once, years ago, lankier than now), with a handsome head and a cast to it that would seem arrogant but for the seamings of humor and good humor in the face and a kindliness and courtesy of manner that in all likelihood would have seemed a bit old-fashioned even when he was a young boy. He was little more than a boy when I first knew him—when he and Cal Lowell came from Kenyon College to be graduate students at LSU. They were both in a graduate seminar of mine connected with Elizabethan non-dramatic literature.

Taylor read widely and dutifully and never opened his mouth without uttering a shrewd perception or wry criticism—all from the slightly askew angle of vision which is his and his alone. He was, in short, a unique asset to an ambitious little group who could appreciate him. Meanwhile, I had become acquainted with his fiction and felt that here was genius—or its first cousin. Also a friendship had begun, for talk in that little seminar didn't end with the 6 P.M. bell on Tuesday or Wednesday or whatever day—I forget.

Alas, the seminar was soon to be deprived of the shrewd comments and wry criticisms. With grave kindness, more like a father explaining the facts of life to a young son than like a student walking across the campus in the dusk with a professor, Peter tactfully explained that graduate work was not for him. He made the blow very soft for me and tried to absolve me of blame. He had to be a writer, he said, and he had to put all his eggs in one basket. I knew damned well he was a writer if I'd ever seen one, and I was in no mood to criticize his decision.

*Reprinted from *Shenandoah* 28, no. 2 (Winter 1977):8–10, by permission of the publisher.

Peter stayed on at LSU a while to give our little community the benefit of his tales, his charm, his warmth, his wit. And of course, became a writer—and a gift of God to the *Southern Review* in which he published his first three stories for the common reader. Then more stories, and the war.

In the years after the war, our paths crossed less frequently, but happily (to speak for myself), and my admiration for his stories and satisfaction in his growing reputation knew no diminution. And one visit to Kenyon, on my way back to New England after taking my tiny daughter South to exhibit her to my aged father, Peter's little daughter gave mine (only 3 months old) her first doll—still treasured.

Peter had become the full-fledged professional, even if now, like so many other writers of the age (Jarrell, Lowell, Barth, Roth, Bellow, etc.) he was professoring, too, usually with a farm somewhere in the background or a house in a country town within striking distance of the academic seat. Where has he taught? Kenyon, University of Ohio, Woman's College of North Carolina, University of Virginia, Harvard— I am forgetting something of his restless life.

Once, before he taught at Harvard, he and I met there as fellow-members of the regularly invited committee to "inspect" the Department of English. The "inspection" ended with a dinner, grand and well lubricated. This being the time of our "involvement" in Southeast Asia and of most rancorous argument, conversation ran high. One local professor turned to Peter and said: "This isn't like the war you fought in—when you had a cause."

Peter replied: "Oh, I don't know. I didn't want to fight in that war either, and wrote a firm letter to my draft board telling them so, to count me out. Months passed, but nothing happened. Not a word. Later, when I was in Memphis, I dropped by the draft board office to see what was happening, and to my great surprise, the secretary turned out to be a beautiful high-school sweetheart. After we got through hugging and kissing and turning back the clock, I edged round to the letter.

"'Oh that,' she said with supreme condescension, 'I knew you didn't really mean a word you said. So I just threw it in the waste basket.' You can't win, I figured, so I put on the uniform."

I remember that Peter never fired a shot in anger, and spent the whole war saving the United States by reading and rereading the works of Trollope. Which I regard as a more suicidal activity than going over the top in World War I.

The Writer

That's one Peter. The other I think of is the splendid, beautiful, cunning writer, who has made a certain segment of American life his own forever, who writes stories that are singularly and subtly his own, and who lately has been writing another kind of story which I find very exciting and perhaps revolutionary. If I had to name the few writers of our century who have captured a true and original world in the story form, I should have Peter's name very high on a very short list. And he is at the height of his powers.

I said there are two Peters. But I can think of neither without remembering Eleanor, with that grave beauty on the face and on the printed page.

Peter Taylor

*Allen Tate**

I was Peter's first college English teacher, but I found I could not teach him anything so I asked him to leave the class after about two weeks. The simple truth is that he did not need to know anything I could teach him. He had a perfection of style at the age of 18 that I envied.

I do not think he owes very much to anybody. If the South has produced a Chekhov, he is Peter Taylor. Literary theories or other abstractions do not blur his vision. I can claim to have helped him in other ways. I introduced him to his wife. If that makes me a matchmaker, I am very proud of the results. Eleanor is a gifted poet and I think they collaborate by not showing each other their work.

It's not possible that Peter Taylor is 60 years old. [Editor's Note: This essay was published as a commemoration of Taylor's sixtieth birthday.] Why, it was only yesterday he walked into my classroom.

*Reprinted from *Shenandoah* 28, no. 2 (Winter 1977):10, by permission of the publisher.

Peter and Randall

Mary Jarrell[*]

Like Chekhov, Peter was an element of Randall's make-up, whom you were indoctrinated with and if the name of "the best fiction-writer around" wasn't as familiar to you as the other you got an astonished stare from Randall and felt dismissed as a tasteless, ill-read boor.

They met in the thirties at Vanderbilt in the aura of Allen and Red and Mr. Ransom. And they became *real* friends after the war when they were two literate Tennesseans in the wilds of New York. Before my time, they'd summered at Cape Cod and weathered a winter or two in a duplex in Greensboro where nobody mowed the lawn but Peter; where a Mahler symphony on the Jarrell side came through the walls to the Taylor side with perfect fidelity; but, also where Randall praised and criticized and conferred invaluably with Peter about *A Woman of Means*, some of his stories, and literature in general.

In the fourteen years after I met Peter he owned nine houses to our one, and rented at least six villas and flat in Europe to our one. At the same time he'd seriously considered, corresponded-about, and nearly got twice that number; and read ads for, driven by, and fantasized over twice as many more. Peter was a House Man. Randall was a Car Man. and Eleanor and I followed their bents. The Jarrells thought the Taylors were a kind of "Main Chance" for aging houses. There they were, we said, two *hot* writers who kept taking on some old house plagued with sinking land-fill or ceiling problems, or both; and making it well, releasing it and taking on another.

On the flyleaf of our copy of *Miss Lenora When Last Seen* Peter wrote: "With love from the Fisher Park Taylors and especially the head of the house (meaning the one who likes houses best)." He sympathized with houses, we thought, the way Chekhov sympathized with women. He knew every shade of their social status the way he knew every accent

[*]Reprinted from *Shenandoah* 28, no. 2 (Winter 1977):28–34, by permission of the publisher.

from East to Middle to West *Tenn*-essee. And "exploring" the country-side with him, Peter could see one one-time *mar*-velous End-chimney house or Center-hall house in every forlorn old farm-dwelling stuffed with hay.

When Randall talked literature, composers, or painters Peter listened and absorbed. When Peter talked St. Louis, his grand-*faw*ther, or Parties we listened and thousands of *New Yorker* dollars were thrown to the winds. If Peter weren't writing or scraping paint it seemed to us he craved parties as much as Randall detested them. If it was one of the Taylor's parties, we certainly went, but Randall would grumble, "Peter likes too many people." We liked too few. At the Party, Randall—worn and dehydrated from a blazing afternoon on the tennis court—collapsed on the sofa, consumed a gallon of orange juice and contributed as little as possible socially. On the other hand, Peter—who, likely as not, had spent the blazing afternoon laying the brick walk up to his front steps—looked showered, flanneled and radiant; in love with the party, and hoping it would last all night.

"Give me parties by the aesthetic method," was what Randall said when referring to parties recollected in moments of tranquility when we had Peter all to ourselves. This was often in the evening when we were rocking on the dark veranda of "the old Office" in Monteagle, or perhaps in the porch swing behind the wisteria vine at Fisher Park. Time flew as Peter presented Randall—sparing him the strain of actual encounter—with the highlights from parties with the Bishop of Sewanee, or the dowager Mrs. Polk from the Delta, or Irene Castle who he reported was raising Great Pyrenees.

Peter's party stories usually had a sprinkling of what my St. Louis mother called "prominent people" compared with "nonentities," and Peter's enchantment with these was to Randall both appealing and naive. Peter's account of his thrilling discovery at the Royal Court Theatre that he was seated directly back of Princess Margaret brought an eons-older smile to Randall's face. Never mind, I thought, Princess Margaret would have thrilled me, too; and it was all due to this "weakness" of Peter's that we wound up that summer in Levanto sipping Negronis on the Louis Seize furniture of the hand-kissing Baron Massola.

Except for Peter the Jarrells would have stuck in their Cape Cod rut forever, I think, but one spring in Columbus changed all that. The Taylors were living in their Twenties Spanish with-the-powder-room-under-the-stairs and Jarrells were on one of those hectic, over-programmed, university-paid lecture trips that Peter and Randall wangled in order to see each other. These were better than nothing, we all agreed, but Randall called them "scrappy visits that hardly count." Between cafeteria lunches and cutting across parking lots we'd catch up on Cal, Allen, Jean, Red, Cleanth, Katherine Anne, Robie, the Ransoms, et al., but there was too little time for James or Tolstoy or Proust.

On our last morning there—I seem to remember having waffles and coffee in the breakfast nook—Peter had just said, "I know people should never bore other people with their dreams," and told us one (which certainly didn't bore old dream analyzers like us for one second) and then suddenly remembered the important news that the Taylors had rented a villa with French doors and fruit trees in Buonassola, and why didn't we come, too? Before we could say Yes, No, or Where's that? Peter produced from the quadrant of his brain that controlled Ril Estate a roof garden flat for us in nearby Levanto, with a little English library, a half-day maid, and a dressing *cabina* at the beach with a private plot of sand and *um*-brella. We took it.

That summer Peter's and Randall's friendship expanded its capacity to seven. There were Peter/Eleanor and Randall/Mary; also, their Katie and my Beatrice; also, their Petey, "our" youngest member, who called time on us to eat, to go home, and to talk pterodactyls with him or the Arch of Titus. Every time Peter softly cautioned him, "Now, Petey, don't be a pest," it evoked from my childhood my mother's, "Now Mary, don't make a scene."

Because of Petey we rarely met at night, and because of the writers we rarely met in the morning; but we often met for picnics and swims and tea at the *pasticceria*. We explored La Spezia where Shelley drowned, Chiavari where those spindly chairs are made, and Rapallo where The Taylors had once rented a house.

In Rapallo some of us longed to see the sights by white-fringed *carozza* which some of us thought Absurd and some of us feared was too much for the house, but all acquiesced. No sooner had we wedged and layered our seven selves into the *carozza* than we realized Rapallo was all hills. At once, those who'd felt Absurd felt increasingly so and sat in uneasy silence while the horse labored upward, ever upward to The House Where The Taylors Stayed. Then, on the downward sprint, those who'd feared for the horse feared even more for themselves and clutched leather staring starkly straight ahead all unmindful of the great estates whizzing past where Peter said Pound and Lawrence and Beerbohm had stayed.

It was a summer of Chekhovian vignettes. In the *ristorante*, all of us starving and impatient except Peter patiently diverting Petey with a car-chase "and they all came to grief on the old Rocky Road" complete with cartoons on the paper napkins. In the little English library, Beatrice on her couch looking up from "Major Barbara" and asking Katie on her couch what was happening in her book. And Katie answering, "Um . . . well . . . oh . . . Christian and Hopeful have just gotten to Doubting Castle and are talking to Giant Despair." And Peter and I sunning ourselves on the little mole looking toward the beach at bearded Randall, browned and bared to the waist, animatedly going over the final manuscript of Eleanor's poems for *Wilderness of Ladies*. Like characters in a silent movie Randall read, head down and then exclaimed, head up, and then bent toward his colleague admiringly, and talked to her in a fiercely determined way: Eleanor, knees under, and speechless, gazed out to sea smiling her half-believing, half-embarrassed smile.

Meanwhile back at the mole, Peter and I—trying tactfully to stay away a little longer—had completely run out of conversation and were mindlessly talking about Eloise Hoblitzelle whom I had never met but shared a legacy with, and whom Peter had never met but thought he knew of because "Hoblitzelle is a good name in St. Louis." I'd begun to think Peter must feel as if he were stuck with me at a dance and it was a welcome sight when Randall stood up on the sand and waved us in. How we all blended that summer like one household at two addresses. How bereft the Jarrells were at the end when the Taylors set off for Rome with stars in their eyes and a dozen new abodes ahead to contemplate.

Our copy of *Happy Families Are All Alike* is inscribed: "To Randall and Mary and Beatrice with love from all of us—and let's start making plans for next summer." Peter made them for Monteagle and found us Rhodes' End near the Lytles that summer, and the Ewing house near the tennis court the next.

Another summer we went Antioch on his account. It was a little out of our style but when the Summer School Dean told us Peter would be there Randall accepted. Actually, Antioch wasn't quite in their style either. In the first place, Peter and Randall "made it a rule" not to teach in the summers. In the second place, their family of four, and ours of three (plus cats), was not accustomed to graduate student housing. But the final flaw, and perhaps the worst, was that the only place to eat in Antioch was The Lemon Drop with its Dieter's Plate instead of some sway-backed clapboard home on a dirt road—that Peter always knew about in *Tenn*-essee—where a pair of widowed sisters served *mar*velous meals. As time wore on we wondered more and more why in the world Peter had wanted to come to this place, and when the mood seemed right we asked. Peter looked at us in amazement and cried out, "We? We only came because the Summer School Dean said you were going to be here." When he wrote in *A Long Fourth* for us he said: "For Randall and Mary with love from Peter and Eleanor on the night of August 28 at Antioch!" with Antioch underlined three times.

My mother used to say, "Peter has such a way about him" meaning what St. Louis used to call "an engaging manner" and what the Jarrells called "being irresistible." We knew that inside *our* Peter Taylor was the solitudinous writer, the Tolstoy reader and the pater familias even though on the outside he seemed all youth and charm and the darling of a prominent family. People liked that. People would open up for Peter and tell all, or as Randall said, "eat out of his hand." He could talk their language, and we'd hear him threatening as they might to go on a diet; or give up *cigarettes;* or write a letter to the newspaper; except when *he* talked that way it was interesting.

For instance, Peter believed his body had a "good" side and a "bad" side, as if you drew an imaginary vertical line down the middle of him both halves would be different. Well, so is everybody's. But Peter's were different—he claimed—because the "good" side was always perfectly OK and the "bad" side always got the sinus trouble, the ear-ache and the sprained ankle.

Another superstition he had that Randall could never cure him of was that a wolf could mate with a dog. Peter was always coming up with some story about "a dog that was part wolf" or was it part bear? And once or twice Randall wanted to take exception to this and argue it out but in time he let Peter get away with it and would only shake his head and say, "Peter Bell. You're a scream."

Part of the reason he was such good company on trips was that he didn't "overlook" and was never "indifferent" and somehow maintained a kind of sparkling *interest* in all the little life around us. We'd hear him telling Katie he'd have to go in debt again for her allowance, but he'd pay it all back the very minute the *New Yorker* check came and for her to keep track of it. And then he'd go on with such genuine *interest*, "You are keeping track of it, aren't you, Katie? How much do I owe to date?" And when Katie asked, "Mmm . . . Oh . . . Do you mean in lira, Daddy?" Peter said, "Oh, heaven's no! Tell me in dollars, Katie, then it won't be so much."

Another time in the car when all of us were bound for Rutledge Falls or The Old Stone Fort, Randall and I got teasing about some signs nailed on trees that said, Pop Taylor's EATS or Taylor and Taylor Wreckers or Taylor and Son Cesspools and Peter said, smiling, "Yes, those are all relatives of mine." And when Randall and I laughed and laughed, he said, not laughing at all, "But they rilly are. All the Taylors in *Tenn*-essee *are* related. All kin."

With my mother, Peter again would seem especially interested as I'd watch him talk and listen with her in the lamplight having what he'd later say was "a fascinating conversation" about Mary Institute, and porte-cocheres and the Veiled Prophet's Ball. And all the while seventy years would slip away until my mother—like Proust's grandmother—had the face of a girl again. In a book he gave to her, Peter wrote: "To Mrs. MacAdams and our very complicated relationship—that is, to my favorite mother of a friend and/or to the mother of my favorite friends."

Now, as I finish, I wonder—as I never did at the time—why this friendship worked? Literature is undoubtedly what brought them together. But after that, they were on their own. Why *were* they so close? They weren't much alike. Peter was a romantic and Randall was an intellectual. Peter loved England and drank whiskey; Randall loved Germany and drank Riesling. Peter had children and Randall had cats. Peter quoted people and played bridge. Randall quoted books and played tennis. Peter wrote fiction and Randall wrote poetry.

Of course that last distinction may have helped the friendship on both sides. To be perfectly honest, I doubt if Randall would have felt quite so cosy if the *New Yorker* were continuously bringing out Peter's *poetry*. And another safeguard, perhaps, was that the temperature of their friendship was like Goldilock's porridge—not too hot, not too cold, but just right. Nobody was ever a pest and nobody made a scene.

Today I've come to think that great friendships are a mystery as Chekhov says love is. That this one did not make old bones does not wipe out the fact that for a time—a rather long time—two people saw the best and not the worst in each other. Though it came to an end, and can never be repeated, it did exist—like our youth and our innocence—and so can be, for occasions like this, blissfully and briefly recaptured.

Like Nothing Else
In Tennessee

*Stephen Goodwin**

The word "Tennessee," Peter Taylor says, rises up off the page and springs at him. He claims he can spot it instantly even on a page of the *Times*, and then he asks, "Do you think that's conceited?" It runs in the Taylor family to identify with Tennessee, and Peter's worldly fore-bears, judges and politicians and soldiers, bought and sold big chunks of it. When he talks about them, they sound hard-headed and high-handed, complacent and alarming like those cigar-smoking gents in "Two Pilgrims." They know Tennessee, and it is theirs. Peter, I can't help thinking, is the boy in that story who drives them across the breadth of the state until finally, exasperated by their proprietary rem-iniscences, he bursts out and tells them that the country side is god-forsaken. The two pilgrims drone right on. In their Tennessee, to borrow a line from Walker Percy, everyone but a fool knows what the good life is and everyone but a scoundrel leads it. The Tennessee of Peter's stories is also genteel, but just outside the pale of propriety stand the fools and the scoundrels, the fancy women and drunkards, Mr. Speed and Aunt Munsie, and they have to be reckoned with. Man-ners are no longer bulwarks but the most susceptible tissues, and Peter has nothing like the baronial confidence of the two pilgrims about the security of *his* dominion.

Still, he must have felt some urge to repel an uncouth trespass when he read, almost ten years ago, the opening pages of a novel which I sent him as part of my application to graduate school at the University of Virginia. The first sentence began, "In my home state of Tennessee . . ." But Peter is generous to students, and he interceded in my be-half. That "Tennessee" must have done it. He told me when I arrived in Charlottesville that he felt as confident as Ford Madox Ford when

*Reprinted from *Shenandoah* 28, no. 2 (Winter 1977):53–58, by permission of the publisher.

he glanced at my manuscript—Ford, who is notorious for his prompt decisions—but I'm sure that he was apprehensive during our first meeting: there I sat, Peter's for at least a year, another young man determined to write, and it quickly came out that I'd never even lived in Tennessee. It was a hot September afternoon, and Peter's office was stuffy; he was conservatively and warmly dressed in tweeds and a tie. I thought his manner was slightly formal, but when I told him that I had given up that novel, that I was there to write stories, he was relieved. At Kenyon, he said, he wrote poems for Mr. Ransom—his tactful way of telling me that he would prefer me to write what he knew best. He was wild to write when he went to Kenyon, and of course he'd had to try his first stories. One of them was "A Spinster's Tale," and Robert Lowell, a classmate, teased him unmercifully about it. He accused Peter of being prim and puritanical, and to prove him wrong, Peter sat down and wrote the first sentence of "The Fancy Woman."

"He wanted no more of her drunken palaver," I said. Peter was tickled that I could quote the sentence, but I'd read the story not long before and it's a memorable line, a nearly perfect alexandrine; with its balance and composure, with that "palaver" resonating like the title with just the proper shudder of disdain, the sentence wasn't prim but it wasn't bawdy either. It seemed to me wonderfully discreet, as Peter himself was discreet during that first meeting. I was his student, after all, and we had our own properties to observe, and even though I wasn't from Tennessee, even though I didn't have any undergraduate stories like "The Fancy Woman" to show him, Peter had made me feel, without being chummy or confiding, that he wanted me there and that it was possible for me to do good work (having Peter as your writing teacher must be like having Ted Williams as your batting coach; they make it sound so easy—and of course it is if you have their talent).

I was one of twenty or so students in his fiction writing class, and we studied him, as students always study their teachers. One of the women in the class was fascinated by his beautiful, well-made clothes, his tweeds and neck-scarves and English shoes; she was fascinated because he was so obviously not a dandy or a snob, and one day it came to her he looked like an elegant mountaineer. She was right. Peter has broad hands and large, expressive features; he has a comfortable walk as if he is always moving down a slight incline. His face is lined but calm and open, and his eyes are a light blue; my classmate found it easy to imagine him on a ridge, wearing buckskins and resting on his musket, gazing into Appalachian distances. That seemed romantic to me, but I do believe, as Bellow does, that landscape shapes faces, and hill people acquire the look of their hills, ocean people of their oceans. Peter does look like Tennessee.

He told us on the first day of class that he was neither a disciplinarian nor an inspirationalist. He never lectured to us; he couldn't have. The lecturer is usually something of a self-infatuate, and he must at least succeed for an hour in supposing that his audience is one united body, a single consciousness attuned to his own. Peter was always aware of the twenty of us spread out in a grim classroom that was much too large, trying to sprawl in desks as rigid as upturned shoe lasts. He sat behind the raised wooden desk at the front of the room and read us our own stories—"throwing them to the wolves," I've heard him call this, but he was never savage or impatient. His method was to say the most generous and admiring things he could about our work, no matter how thin and pawky. He was never insincere, either, because the story he praised was not the story on the page, the visible text, but the bewitching story we'd conceived but hadn't been able to write. He'd talk about the way characters looked or spoke or dressed, putting words into their mouths and inventing their gestures. He might say, "This character should fall in love," or something more devious, "I kept expecting there would be trees in this story," and when he did venture a suggestion in that way, the deficiency immediately seemed obvious. And though his comments nearly always had to do with the story's surface, and he never spoke of "form" or "theme," it was always clear that important activity was going on below the surface. He seemed to think of a story as a net to be cast wide and dragged deep until it filled with startling, shining life. As you hauled it in, the concentrated shapes began to show—but you could never raise your net from the water full of trophies and specimen, for its lines, after all, were illusions.

When Peter didn't have the heart to read us our own prose, he read stories by the writers he loves, Lawrence and Turgenev and Chekhov and Frank O'Connor. He read quietly, without emphasis, imposing as little as possible on the text. When he finished, he'd close the book— they were always cloth, never paperbacks, and he treated them with great respect—and wonder for a moment what he could say to make us know what we'd just heard. For Peter stories are a mode of under-standing, *the* mode; to try to understand them critically was to depart from the source. He didn't want us to analyze but to recognize and revere what James called "felt life," and most of us, with the busy clever minds of graduate students, were slow to grasp the lesson that seemed so vague but was in fact the most rigorous lesson of all. Peter would go back over the story, singling out passages and *imagining* them for us, making us not critics but collaborators.

Peter was living that year in the house Faulkner had owned when he was the writer at Virginia; he's since moved into a large frame house formerly owned by someone called Mister Hank, where he says he feels more comfortable. In between he owned an 18th century farmhouse which had an outbuilding he intended to convert from a storage facility for oriental rugs into a small, intimate theater. These have been his three main residences, but in ten years he's also bought and sold a cabin in the Blue Ridge, two farms in Albermarle County, one or two places in Sewanee, and most recently, sight unseen, a place in Key West. He has at different times contemplated taking apartments in Cambridge, Washington, and London, and he and his wife Eleanor subscribe to local papers in several different parts of the country in order to keep abreast of the real estate. He says, with a magisterial flourish, that he considers it his duty to the Taylor family to keep turning property over. There are imposing, full-length Taylor portraits in the house in Charlottesville, but Peter's own portrait is casual; he is seated at an outdoor table with Eleanor and their two children. Some of the furniture in the house is Taylor furniture too, and when I first went there as a student—Peter often invites students, and not just to the usual awkward soirees as the conferring of a privilege, but to the real grown-up affairs—I knew how Goldilocks felt in the house of the Three Bears: everything was either too formidable or too dainty. For Peter and Eleanor, everything is just right; their houses, all of them, are among the few houses I know which seem the natural environment of their occupants. And Peter, at home, is a presence of relaxed, benevolent gaiety. He dominates, though never in an assertive way. He says witty things, but he's entirely free of the malice and self-aggrandizing instinct of most wits. He tells stories, but they come tumbling out every which way; he's not the polished raconteur that his two pilgrims were. Though he's delighted when opinions are in play, he's no debater either; he doesn't cultivate differences. Spending an evening in his company is like reading his stories: it resembles ordinary life, but somehow it's not a bit boring.

Last summer Peter and a friend, another former student, drove over to my place in western Virginia. We all spent a shady afternoon talking, and Peter told us that he was at last writing a story about his grandfather. As he described it—his grandfather and his grandfather's law partner were kidnapped by a gang of hooded riders, and as the partner was hung, his grandfather dove into a lake and took cover behind a log, which, in the early light, the kidnappers fired upon and allowed to drift away, mistaking it for his dead body—I wondered how Peter would write a yarn of adventure and murder. And when he told us that his grandfather then wandered for days and suffered hallucinations, imagining that the earth opened in craters and fissures beneath his feet as if the earthquake a century earlier was being repeated, I was as a loss. It was as strange to me as if Henry James had just said he was going to write *The Sound and the Fury*. I'd heard Peter say rebellious things before; he threatened after the death of his mother, Katherine Taylor Taylor, to unmake part of the Tennessee he'd created by writing a novel set in "*not*-Memphis." On this afternoon he said, "I can write all the stories I know, because now everyone in them is dead."

When the afternoon cooled off we persuaded Peter to change out of his flannels and blazer and we all swam in a mountain creek full of cold springs that rose through the stones on the bottom. Peter remembered a deep cold pool where he and Eleanor used to swim, the Devil's Bathtub. He was in a genial, acquisitive mood that afternoon; he wanted to buy all the houses he saw, and as we were eating in the garden, watching the shadows drift down the mountains, he said that he was reminded of Tennessee, the highest compliment he could pay to the place. After dinner we went inside and somehow, perhaps because we'd come from the garden, we began a game of vegetable charades. Peter hollowed his cheeks in an inspired imitation of a peanut, which we all guessed, but his triumph was a flailing approximation of mustard greens. Mustard greens—who but Peter would have thought of it? Not one of us had ever seen mustard greens, but he twisted his face in such a perfect scansion of mustard, and he was so alive, root and leaf, that we were sure we would recognize them anywhere.

A few weeks ago I read "In the Miro District," the story he told us about. It wasn't what I expected—that is, it is Peter through and through. It begins in the most affable, natural way; a patient speaker, slightly amused by the old-fashioned quality he detects in his own voice, finds himself speculating on that "antediluvian Tennessee" in which he grew up. And while it's the grandfather's story, it is the grandson, Peter, who has custody of it. The grandfather, for all his exploits, is a formidable old bore whose stories, told over and over again in the same rehearsed phrases, have become an oppression to the boy. In a daring reversal, the grandson, eighteen years old and sublimely drunk, turns the tables and afflicts the grandfather with the stories he has memorized. It is a stunning scene, for Peter makes us acknowledge that the stories we know by heart, the stories which contain our past, do not always join us; they may divide us, generation from generation. The telling of them is our passage into the freedom of our own lives.

An Interview with
Peter Taylor

*Stephen Goodwin**

[Stephen] Goodwin: Most of the people that you knew at Kenyon were poets. Did this have any effect on you?

[Peter] Taylor: It had a very strong and lasting effect on me. Mr. Ransom was teaching at Kenyon while I was there, and so was Randall Jarrell, and my classmates, like Lowell, were almost exclusively interested in poetry. I think poets talked more about technical problems in those days, about meter and form, and they insisted upon closeness and structure and texture—those are words that they used a great deal—in writing. It's probably responsible for my turning into a short story writer rather than a novelist.

Goodwin: Did you write any poetry of your own?

Taylor: My ego required that I write poetry just to make an impression on that group. My interest in poetry had consisted of Whittier and such, which I had learned by heart as a boy, but at Kenyon I set about reading poetry of all kinds. At one point, Lowell and I decided that we were going to get out an anthology together and we went through centuries of poetry. And I wrote poetry for nearly the whole time I was there. The first thing I ever published, the first thing I was ever paid for, was a poem in the *Kenyon Review*. Mr. Ransom rather insisted on my writing poetry. I remember a piece I wrote for him, a story with a poem in it—you know how you want to get everything in when you're beginning to write. Well, Mr. Ransom read the story and returned it with a note at the top: *B* for the story, *A* for the poem. Mr. Ransom just wouldn't pay much attention to my fiction; Jarrell was the only one there who did. He was much more interested, even then, in characters in poetry than any of the others were. But even though Mr. Ransom

Reprinted by permission from *Shenandoah* 24, no. 2 (Winter 1973):3–20.

condescended to fiction then—I think his attitude changed later, while he was editing the *Kenyon Review*—and insisted that I write poems, I learned a tremendous amount from him. When you're a young person working with a writer, I think that it's best for that time to try to learn what the writer can teach you. Mr. Ransom was a poet, so I wrote poems for him.

Goodwin: There must have been a good deal of competition in this group.

Taylor: I didn't feel that, and I don't think that I just won't admit it. We all wanted to publish, of course, but we weren't just mad for publishing. I think we were more interested in each other's opinion than in the world's opinion. And in any literary clique people are going to have pretty much the same values; they're naturally going to like and admire each other's work if they're congenial, if they're all working on the same level. We did compete in other things, in grades—until I went to Kenyon I really didn't care about grades, but among Lowell and Jarrell and Macauley and John Thompson and all those people, I wanted to be good at what they were good at. I felt, for the first time, that I had found my peers.

Goodwin: Why did you turn back to fiction?

Taylor: I had always been interested in stories. In my family the Southern oral tradition really did persist; my family told stories constantly and talked about the past. But what I most wanted to be, like so many fiction writers, was a painter. My only serious early training was as a painter. I took classes in school and after school. When I went to Kenyon I was still painting; that was my real impulse. . . .

Goodwin: What about Faulkner? Flannery O'Connor once said that all Southern writers have to deal with Faulkner, that to write about the South without knowing your Faulkner was like having your mule and wagon stalled on the track with the Dixie Limited bearing down on you. Do you think of Faulkner as an obstacle or as a source?

Taylor: I think that we all ought to get down on our knees every night and thank God for Faulkner. He is the master; he taught us all to observe our own world, the benefits of observing it closely. Some writers make breakthroughs, and all writing has a great surge after that; everybody benefits from it. What gets borrowed or stolen doesn't matter, because a good writer always adds something, makes his particular mark. I'm not at all ashamed when somebody accuses me of stealing.

I have stolen unconsciously, and I admit it. If you love a Chekhov or a Katherine Anne Porter or a Faulkner story so much, you can't help wanting to do something like it. You often will do something like it and more, and why worry about it? If the thief goes farther or in a different direction, what could be a greater compliment to the writer he stole from?

I don't think Eudora Welty could have written without Faulkner; by the same token, Eudora Welty made it possible for Flannery O'Connor to write. I think Flannery found things in certain stories of Eudora's, stories like "The Petrified Man" and "Keela, the Outcast Indian Maiden," that she could take and make her own. This is not to say that she imitated Eudora, any more than Eudora imitated Faulkner, but that Eudora introduced the kinds of subjects in her fiction, and handled them with a kind of comic sensibility, that created a field for Flannery.

Goodwin: What writers other than Southern writers do you look to as your master?

Taylor: Chekhov, of course, and Turgenev; I read all of Turgenev and really felt closer to him than to Chekhov. And Joyce, Frank O'Connor, D. H. Lawrence. I read Henry James and Proust and Thomas Mann. As a matter of fact, I always thought I had been influenced by Mann, and I wrote several stories that I believed were very much in the manner of Mann. Nobody else ever noticed it. "Skyline" is one of my Mann stories which is so far undetected. And it certainly doesn't seem like Mann to me, nowadays.

Goodwin: How do you actually, physically, do your writing?

Taylor: I don't use any outlines or notes. I just begin with the first sentence, first paragraph, and by the time I have a page or two—and that may take some while, at my rate—the margins are just crawling with things I've jotted down. What happens later in the story—the incidents, characterization, lines of dialogue—often comes from these messages I've written myself at the beginning. I don't mean to say that the whole story reveals itself in that first burst of energy, in those first pages. I wish it did. I usually have to wait for a second inspiration before I know how a story will end. The story may have taken a direction I hadn't foreseen, or I may have gotten interested in a different aspect of it, or the original may simply go bad—all sorts of things can divert that first impulse.

Goodwin: Do you then revise the first portion of the story?

Taylor: Not unless I have to. I try to hedge my bets. Of course I have to revise sometimes, and sometimes I've had to throw out an entire story. . . .

Goodwin: Are many of your stories based on stories that you heard at home or elsewhere? On characters that you knew?

Taylor: There was a period when I tried to see if I could make every speech in the dialogue in a story one that I had heard somewhere. And in some stories—like "Their Losses"—practically every word in even the smallest speech is one that I heard. And "A Spinster's Tale" is right out of my mother's mouth. My mother was rather prim and puritanical—"old-maidish," we used to say, at least she had that side of her—and that story is really hers. Her mother died when she was fourteen, and she was right there in the house; there was a baby that died; the dreams in the story are her dreams, and there was a real Mr. Speed. The language in the story was my mother's too—it's more Victorian, more elevated than the language in most of my stories.

Lowell always teased me about that story. We were still at Kenyon when I wrote it, and he told me that *I* was prim and puritanical, that I didn't know anything about the world, that there wasn't enough of the roughness of life in my stories. So I vowed I'd show him, and I sat down and wrote the first sentence of "The Fancy Woman": *He wanted no more of her drunken palaver.* I had no idea where I was going from there, and then suddenly a whole story based on someone I knew, a father with two boys, just came to me. The story took over—well, it wasn't quite as simple-minded as that. . . .

. . . The reason I could use dialogue word for word in those stories of mine, stories like "Their Losses" or "Two Pilgrims," is that those stories were old stories, stories which had been told over and over again. Those speeches stayed the same time after time, and you know that when a story like that doesn't change, there must be something in it. By the time those stories came down to me, those speeches had been refined so that they revealed a great deal about the people who spoke them. So I didn't have to change a word.

Goodwin: Are any of your stories invented from whole cloth?

Taylor: I've worked some stories out just the way you'd work out a theorem. I spent months on "Venus, Cupid, Folly, and Time," working out the theme of it, although I suppose I could probably mention somebody as the original of every character in that story. "Miss Lenora When Last Seen" is another story that I constructed just as deliberately as I could. Those two, "Venus, Cupid, Folly, and Time" and "Miss Lenora," are for me complete allegories, although they may not be for the rest of the world. I don't think that matters very much. I was shocked to read what "The Dead" was supposed to mean to Joyce—and once you know all the secrets, your reading of the story is never the same, you're no longer innocent. Joyce may have required all that scaffolding, but that's not what makes the story a great story for the reader. . . .

Goodwin: You and Jarrell taught together at Greensboro for several years. Did he have any influence on your stories?

Taylor: A great deal. I learned a lot about fiction from Randall. During those years he read my stories and made many suggestions, many of which I followed. He was very sympathetic, as people might not have suspected, to the Southern quality of my stories. He urged me to write about the South, to record it. He used to say, "This is all going to be gone in a few years. It has to be written down now. You're writing not just for literature but for posterity." He wanted a very naturalistic tone in the stories—he objected to my more severe stories, the more schematic stories like "Venus, Cupid, Folly, and Time," although he later came around to thinking it was one of my best. . . .

. . . It may be that a writer's most important possession, after his talent, is his sense of belonging to a time and place, whatever the disadvantages or injustices or cruelties of that time and place may be. The writer isn't going to change the world, or at least I'm not; I've had to write about the world as I found it. . . .

Goodwin: You said that you were a reader of Lawrence. What do you think of his handing of sex?

Taylor: I remember reading *Lady Chatterly's Lover* when it first came out. The bad words had all been left out. It was very exciting. His *blank* and her *blank*. There's real suggestion for you. But I don't think that that book, for all the time they spend in bed, has as much genuine, intense sexuality as some of the other novels and the stories where the sex is much more implicit. Of course, Lawrence at his best, in his really great stories like "The White Stocking" and "The Horse-Dealer's Daughter," is very much more than a sex writer. He's one of the real masters of the short story. I've always thought so, and I've always been puzzled by people who wonder how I can like Lawrence and Joyce or

Lawrence and Chekhov at the same time. Why shouldn't I? Lawrence and Joyce are both masters, even if they are poles apart. When you're reading one, you accept the truth of his view; when you read the other, you accept his truth. It's absurd to think that one somehow cancels out the other. . . .

Goodwin: Which of your stories are your own favorites?

Taylor: I like different stories for different reasons. I think that "Venus, Cupid, Folly, and Time" and "Miss Lenora" are among the best stories I've written, but that may be because I worked so hard on them. I worked them out systematically, I assembled characters and situations to make them work as stories, I knew exactly what I was saying. After all the time I put in—I spent months and months on "Venus, Cupid, Folly, and Time"—I feel I have to like those stories. And then I like other stories which came very easily, almost like memoirs, because they seem so natural as stories. "A Spinster's Tale" may be one of my best, but I hate to admit it; it was written right at the beginning, and no one likes to think he hasn't gotten better. *"Je Suis Perdue"* is one of my favorites and that story just happened that way. Katie, my daughter, was the little girl who got lost in a movie theatre in Paris. When she called out to me, I didn't recognize her voice because she was calling in French. She was calling, *"Je suis perdue,"* and I didn't really pay attention to her—I didn't know any French children. That story was one of Randall's favorites too. He even noticed that in the story the little girl uses the feminine *perdue*, with an *e*, but in the title the word is masculine, because it's the father who's lost.

Goodwin: Can you say why you've concentrated so on the short story, why you've written only one short novel?

Taylor: It may all go back to my training with Mr. Ransom. I still feel that everything in a work of art must be functional, must contribute, must be working. I'm bored by novels that do less with a chapter than a short story does with a sentence. In fact, I have to confess that I find most novels tedious. More than half of the contemporary novels that I read could have been done more effectively as stories. I really don't like to read any novels except great novels, novels that absolutely have to be novels. . . . [With] nearly everything I've written, I've thrown away as much as I finally kept. . . .

Goodwin: You've written several plays recently. Are you more interested now in drama than in narrative fiction?

Taylor: I'm much more interested in drama, or I will be if I can finish my novel and make a good job of it. I've always felt that the short story is a dramatic form and that it's much more natural for a short story writer to write plays than it is for him to write novels. There are plenty of examples of this: look at Chekhov and Pirandello and the Irish short story writers. Publishers harass short story writers for years, trying to get novels out of them, when a story writer's talent is much more apt to be for plays.

Goodwin: What for you is the difference between a story and a play?

Taylor: Certain subjects are more suited to plays. Some of my plays—"The Death of a Kinsman" is one—were written first as stories and later rewritten as plays, for that reason. There are themes and experiences that fiction simply can't handle convincingly. . . .

Goodwin: It must be very seductive for a writer to see his story materialize before his eyes.

Taylor: The greatest joy is doing something with *people* after all the years of doing things off by yourself, and of course it's fun to see the plays done the way you want them done. I've had the good luck of having several plays produced at Kenyon. . . .

Goodwin: Are you going to abandon stories?

Taylor: I doubt that I'll write many more short stories. I feel that I've done what I want to do as a short story writer. For years I was so absorbed in stories that I didn't think I would ever try to do anything else, but when I start a story now, I know that I can write it. Once you've learned how to do something as well as you can, you just don't care about repeating it. I don't mean to sound conceited, and I don't even mean that I'm satisfied with the stories; but I have a horror of repeating myself, of imitating myself. Some of my favorite writers have done that—Frank O'Connor, for example. He's a marvelous story writer, but after a point he was simply imitating his early stories. It's very difficult to see why the late stories aren't as good as the earlier ones, but they're not. And, as someone said, the story is the young man's form. After *Dubliners*, Joyce didn't want to write any more stories; Katherine Anne Porter, when she had written her stories, went on to other things.

Goodwin: What are your ambitions for your writing? How would you like people to think of it?

Taylor: I've never felt the way many writers do about being professional. My writing is a by-product of my efforts to understand my life; that's what it comes to. I'm always unhappy when I hear someone say, I don't think so-and-so's a very good writer, I've never read anything of his that I like, but he's a real professional. I'd much rather have someone say about me, he's not professional, but he wrote a few things that were really inspired.

Interview with Peter Taylor, March 1, 1986

*J. H. E. Paine**

J. H. E. Paine: The sempiternal Peter Taylor question. How can a writer recognized as the greatest living short story writer in English be so little known? Your career may in some sense be seen as the success story of the college-boy narrator in "1939" who steps out of the shadow of Henry James. Yet your work seems to be read mostly by relatively narrow circles: general readers who have followed your stories in *The New Yorker* over the years, a small group of scholars concerned with Southern fiction, and what one might call "Tennessee readers"—those with ties to your corner of the world who enjoy seeing their region represented in fiction.

Peter Taylor: [A few readers comprise] the most important group to me. That is my numbers of literary friends when I was growing up and through the years. It's what made it possible for me to go on without minding that I had no big reputation as a writer, but I had such wonderful writers as friends just by chance, I suppose, from the time I was very young, that when my books and stories came out, it was sufficient satisfaction to have letters from them and to have their appreciation. They were just extravagant in their praise, primarily Robert Lowell and Randall Jarrell and Jean Stafford and Allen Tate, too, and Robert Penn Warren. They really constituted all that I cared about as a public; I was perhaps mistaken to do that, but I did and I was hardly aware of how little known I was until a few years ago when people began writing—Jonathan Yardley and others—about how little known I was. I knew that I had no big reputation, but I didn't think about it much. I never lived in the center of literary activities. We've always

*From the *Journal of the Short Story in English* 9 (Fall 1987). Copyright 1987 by Presses de l'Université d'Angers. Reprinted with permission.

had a place off somewhere in the country, and our friends, like the Lowells and the Jarrells, would come to visit us, or we'd go to Europe and set up with them. Jarrell and his wife came and set up in Monteagle while we had a cottage there, and we went to Italy with them one summer, and Robert Fitzgerald is a great friend of mine. He would write to me about my stories, and Jarrell and Lowell did, so that I didn't go by the number of the reviews in the periodicals and the *New York Times* and such places. I would get pretty good reviews in those places, but I didn't get much sales for my books, ever.

JHEP: You really had a sense of community.

PT: Yes, I think there was a sense of literary community in that world we lived in. Tate and Warren and Ransom—I had such confidence in them and they were so enthusiastic about my stories, and I thought they were the greatest living writers, and perhaps they were at that time. It was very lucky for me just to be born in their midst, and then to make friends from the early time. Lowell and I were roommates at Kenyon all the way through, and we remained closest friends as long as he lived. He'd come and stay with us weeks at a time, we were that close and wrote to each other always. I have, you know, hundreds of letters from him and from Stafford and lots of others, and from Jarrell about my work.

Jarrell was so funny about the work of his friends. If you published something he didn't like, he just wouldn't speak to you. We were staying together in a little Riviera town one summer and I passed Randall on the street downtown and he turned away and wouldn't speak, and I went to his wife Miriam and said, "What have I said to Randall? What's happened?" And she said, "He doesn't like that last story of yours that came out. That seems terrible, but then he would do the same thing to Lowell—we three were friends—and it got so Lowell would say, "Is he speaking to you?" because he'd get that way, but then if you wrote something he liked, he would write you a long letter about it and that's more valuable than twenty reviews—you got a long letter from Jarrell. . . .

And my wife is a good reader. We've always had a literary society we've lived in, sort of off the beaten track. I'm inclined to say that serious writers didn't used to go so much by the National Book Award, all these prizes, and being a best-seller; none of the writers I knew and thought were the best writers had those prizes, and Lytle and Tate and Warren didn't. Well, Warren had earlier *All the King's Men*, but everybody thought, "What's Red doing having a best seller?" But he did it just by accident, and it's a wonderful book, I think. . . .

. . . I feel very strongly about the use of symbols and symbolic elements in fiction. I think that symbols are there only to support the story and the effect and the belief, and that when you write a story around a symbol having the symbol more important than the story itself, as some modern stories seem to me to be—in fact, I heard some young writer say, "I've got the story all written, but I've just got to put in the symbols"—that seems to me perfectly ridiculous. The symbol should come out of the material. It should be part of the naturalism of the story, and then if they have great symbolic feeling, they are wonderfully effective, but I often don't realize what symbols are in my stories until somebody points them out. . . .

. . . I think writing stories is rather like dreaming, and that if you have a certain temperament or sensibility, you'll have an affinity for certain symbols that will make the story have its impact. I resent a lot of the symbolic values in Joyce and other writers. For instance "The Dead" I think is a wonderful story, a naturalistic story, and I don't deny the interpretations that are put on it, the Christian interpretation on that and on "Araby," but I just sort of shrug and say, "Yes, that's there," and I'm sure it helped Joyce write the story maybe, but I think he wrote a good story almost in spite of those instead of because of them. . . .

. . . I'm crazy about Lawrence's stories, not about his novels. I like one or two novels, but I think the stories are magnificent. They are stories that are very hard to write; that's the hardest kind of story to write, without having any of the props or crutches or anything like that. . . .

. . . As a Southerner you learn from Faulkner; he was in a way the one who taught us how to look at ourselves. And then you looked at yourself as different from him eventually, but still those stories in *These 13* to me are amongst the great stories of the world. I like them much better than the more rhetorical novels and later stories. I like "Was," in *Go Down, Moses*. I like those stories very much. They're the work of genius, but I think "Was" is one of the funniest stories ever written in the world, and I find myself sometimes tempted to steal from it. I think those stories of his are just perfect in *These 13*. I mean "A Rose for Emily" and "That Evening Sun" and those stories. . . .

JHEP: You've managed to suggest Faulkner, which I hadn't really hit upon in a direct way.

PT: But he—we're such different temperaments that our writing has such a different feeling, an attitude toward the South, but you learn where you can learn from other writers who have made use of the context; the context of the stories is very important. . . . That's to me one of the most interesting observations in life now, seeing people in their context. Other people will find it obnoxious in me sometimes, I mean personally—maybe in stories, too—because I at once begin wanting to know who people were and what they were.

It's immensely interesting to me, all the things that make up people's lives, because it's not just one thing, but there's that maybe dominant thing about growing up in Middle Tennessee and observing them and knowing who they were. I was behind a boy in the chow line once overseas during the war and I heard him talking, and I said, "You're from Tennessee," and he said, "Yes," and I said, "You're from Middle Tennessee." He said, "Yes." I said, "You're from Davidson County." . . .

JHEP: I could hardly help notice in your work—this is not the case in the work of other prominent Southern writers—that religion doesn't seem to play a very direct role. . . .

PT: . . . It is perfectly true that I grew up in a family and really a class of people maybe who were not religious and for whom there had been great battles of religion in the past, as there had been great battles of politics. . . .

JHEP: You've studied the drama and you've published a number of plays in addition to your short stories. Could you say just a bit about what prompted you to turn to this second literary vocation?

PT: I wanted to write plays before I wrote stories. I have some very crude things I wrote very young. I'm still working on plays right now. I love to have my plays produced and to go and work with them and rewrite them and everything. I've done it at colleges and at the Barter Theatre in Virginia. I've written a volume of one-act plays, *Presences*, and I enjoyed doing that very much and have been to productions of them at colleges. . . .

JHEP: Did [writing plays] influence the way you wrote your short stories or the way you looked at the short story?

PT: Well, of course I think that the short story is much closer to the play than it is to the novel, that it's a dramatically compressed literary form, and I've pointed out that it's much more natural to go into a play than to go into a novel, generally speaking, for short story writers, and yet short-story writers are pushed into writing novels by the market. Publishers insist. . . . And then J. F. Powers, whom I admire immensely, wrote one novel, under pressure, and it was a good novel, but it was not the inspired thing that some of his stories are. . . .

But generally speaking, I think the *New Yorker* encourages writers. Another thing. I felt so guilty about making so much money from the *New Yorker* for a few years when I was still young and idealistic, I was determined to spend all the money as I made it, and that's why we went to Europe every year for about five years. . . .

JHEP: I was going to put [your use of the digressive retrospective monologue] together with Robert Towers' saying that your work sometimes defies the concentration of the short story, the brevity that's so typical of the short story. I don't know how you reconcile what might be a naturally novelistic mode of narration with the form of the short story. Could it be because of the Southern story-telling tradition?

PT: I think that's some of it, that oral tradition and that I lived in a family of story-tellers. My mother and my grandfather were great raconteurs and anecdotalists, and my father loved so to hear my mother tell stories that he would say over and over, "Tell the one about so-and-so," and the rest of would have heard it so many times, we would wander off, but my father could just listen endlessly to those stories. They were always told with the same phrases, the same vocabulary that came in at just the right moment. . . .

It's partly that, but also it's been one of my interests to see if I can get the effect of a long story, of a novel in a short story suggested by this, and I've consciously done it a lot of the time and enjoyed doing it and not always successfully, I think. Sometimes it's what's wrong with stories, but then sometimes it's worked. After all, Turgenev does it, you know; he's a great one for story-telling that way. . . .

JHEP: Why are women in the psychological and often moral ascendancy over men in your fiction?

PT: Of course, probably I really think they are always, but I think in the South particularly, and particularly the South that I knew growing up; there were old ladies always (I've told you my father was a lawyer and he always had a lot of old ladies whose estates he was looking after) around the house staying with us.

After the Civil War for a long time the woman in many cases was the dominant member of the house. The husbands didn't know what to do. For the men it wasn't the same; there wasn't the authority. They still had a great deal, but I knew more old ladies who spoke with authority than I did old gentlemen, and who were powerful figures. I knew such ladies everywhere and I'm sure they existed in the rest of the South, and to some extent it was a universal thing all over the world in the old days, the spinster aunts who perhaps had a little money and were running things and everybody was hoping to inherit their money and all that. . . .

JHEP: Let me ask you about *"Je Suis Perdu"* because it's one of my favorite stories.

PT: Well, I'm so glad. It's one of my favorites, and it was one of Jarrell's very favorites.

JHEP: Readers sometimes complain about irony, Peter Taylor irony, and you've said practically any short story has to be ironic. But in this story, which I think is one of your most moving, in "Je Suis Perdu," the ironic distance that I keep looking for is attenuated and maybe it's not even there.

PT: Well it's not in the sense that it is in the others, and it is much more autobiographical. Usually the narrator or the principal character in my stories I'm thinking of as somebody else, this somebody I've known or put in. I dissociate myself from it because it's more fun to write it that way. But in this it was my children and my wife and it's almost precisely as it happened. . . . There's a little irony there, but essentially you take the experience directly at the end when he says, "after I found things that I loved even more than myself."

Interview, 1987

James Curry Robison*

James Curry Robison: I gather from Albert J. Griffith's book that your father wanted you to become a lawyer [as his other son did]. Was that the case?

Peter Taylor: Oh yes. That was the great battle of my life. He had always wanted me to be a lawyer. I had marvelous parents. They thought that their four children were the finest, brightest children that ever lived, and my father was sure that I should have been a lawyer. A great mistake it would have been. I wouldn't. I wanted to write. My father wanted me to go to Vanderbilt, where he had gone and become a lawyer, and I wouldn't. I had a scholarship to Columbia and wanted to go there.

So I got a job on the newspaper [in Memphis] and took courses at Southwestern [now Rhodes College]. Allen Tate was teaching there, and he persuaded me that I ought to go to Vanderbilt to study with Ransom. And so I did. Then he left and went to Kenyon, and I followed him.

JCR: But there was a delay in that process. Did your father resist that change as well?

PT: Oh yes, he did, but then I got a scholarship from Kenyon. It was in the Depression, and he wasn't all that affluent. And then he admired Ransom very much. He had been at Vanderbilt at the same time as Ransom.

JCR: Earlier you mentioned painting. Do you still paint?

PT: Not really. I sketch.

JCR: Were there any painters that were particularly influential in your writing or in your view of art?

PT: Well, I was such a beginner, I was enthralled by the Impressionists pretty early in college. The reason I don't paint now is that

*This interview was conducted in Knoxville, Tennessee, on 9 September 1987.

once you get to be pretty good at some art, it's painful to be such a rank amateur at another.

JCR: Many critics have mentioned that your early stories use a feminine point of view, whether first or third person, and that your later stories are told most often by masculine narrators. Were you aware at the time of leaning toward the feminine viewpoint so heavily and then making a switch toward the masculine, or did that just happen?

PT: It sort of happened. I became aware that I was doing it. After the fact it is easy to speculate. I sort of exhausted my [material]. I was terribly aware that women had much more sensibility than men, generally, and it seemed a limiting factor in producing a story's point of view, domestic and all that. What it is for me—writing is always sort of playing around and exploring things, and I exhausted the energy, the impulse, to do that with women's points of view. I began to be more interested in my own life. I began to be more sympathetic with men after a certain point.

You see, when I began "The Spinster's Tale"—that's based very much on my mother, a lot of it; my mother spoke just that way (it's a discovery of evil by a girl)—I was interested in innocence, and I thought of women and girls as being the most innocent. And then I thought, "Well, what if I get a person, not who discovers innocence, but [who] is so corrupted that she cannot recognize innocence when she sees it?" And that's what "The Fancy Woman" is about, in those terms.

To me writing is sort of an argument you have with yourself. You take one point of view and push it and your ideas about. Then you think, "Well, is that really true? I'll try this other way." For instance, I wrote *A Summons to Memphis*, and the book I'm writing now [*To the Lost State*, his novel in progress] comes out of that. It's sort of an antimacho book about a different kind of situation. I sort of argued, "What's the other kind of experience like?" And so in this one I have three more or less macho men (not that I'm antimacho—I'm a great Hemingway admirer), and I have a character who's just the opposite of that. Oh, another thing. I've always wanted to do a book in which there would be a character who suffered from the family. I've always written about people inside the family, and I'm so crazy about the idea of a family and think it's the most important thing in the world for the organization of society and for relationships. What about the people who are outside the family and how they suffer? I began thinking about some of the stories I have heard—country cousins who are awkward and are made fun of in the family. I made such a man the hero in my story [*To the Lost State*]. This has grown out of my arguments with that [in *A Summons to Memphis*]. I can think of a lot of times I have written one story and thought, "Oh, what fun to write it from the opposite point of view."

JCR: The pattern of betrayal in *A Summons to Memphis* and in "Dean of Men"—is there any particular reason you chose that kind of betrayal, the father betrayed by the friend and then inadvertently turning his anger on the family? And that you use it again later?

PT: I don't really know. It's not autobiographical in that sense, as far as my family went. Of course I get angry with my friends when they write someone that seems to be me. My father was most adoring of the brothers and sisters and wanted them to get married. I had seen cases like that, though. It's based somewhat on my father, but just the kernels of the story. My father was betrayed by a friend he thought was a great friend, then for years I had thought about it as a possibility for a story. In old age my father and his friend met at Monteagle [Tennessee], and after not speaking for twenty-five years, they fell on each other. All their friends were dead by that time, and the last few years of their lives they talked on the phone from Nashville to Memphis all the time, after all those years. And we were not allowed to criticize—ever. It was his concern, not ours. Of course the story is really about the narrator, and in the ironic ending, there's still more life to those people fighting it out in Memphis and Cleveland than there is in people going off and living in the book world of New York.

JCR: Earlier you mentioned having been in Allen Tate's class in Memphis. He wrote in a piece in *Shenandoah* in 1977 that, after you had been in his class for two weeks, he was convinced that you knew more than he could teach you, so he asked you to leave the class and do something more productive.

PT: That was rather an exaggeration. He did more for me than anybody. I quarreled with him later; we had a terrible quarrel because he did something horrible. But I forgave him and always said, no matter what awful thing he could have done to me, it was nothing to what he had done for me, when I was young and was his student. He made me feel that writing was so important. He made me feel that art—and writing particularly—was the most important thing in the world to do, and I wasn't sure of that till then. I knew I always wanted to write, but I always felt it was sort of copping out on being a lawyer or something.

I went on to his class and he began telling me I ought to read Chaucer, and I hadn't. So every afternoon we would go and sit under the trees, and he would coach me in reading Chaucer. And he did that with other things and talked to me about literature generally. I went on with that class, that was in the spring, and in the summer I took a novel course under him—a creative writing course, really. He liked the things I would write for the papers in the class. Then I wrote some fiction, and he liked it immensely, and that really set me up and gave me the courage to go on and be a writer.

JCR: How do you account for groups like the Fugitives happening to come together?

PT: That miraculous group at Vanderbilt—there have not been many things like it. Their temperaments and their intellects and all these things, it's such a wonderful coincidence that they turned up at the same time. And it was very wonderful to me, coming along afterward. I knew that the South was what I was interested in, the only thing I knew anything about, and they gave me their ideas to latch onto about what it meant. That's what you're always looking for when you're writing: what does it mean? You like stories. About every fiction writer is somebody who just loves yarns and stories, but that has enough intellect to say they've got to mean something. My mother and father told stories just endlessly, and I wanted to listen. They were good storytellers, but they [the stories] didn't mean anything. Neither of them had any philosophy of life that they were trying to put across. So I was sort of haunted by that. You begin writing saying, "It's got to mean something." If it sticks in your mind, it's like a dream. It probably means something. . . . If you have the right instinct, you will find the thing you want to write.

JCR: I gather, from the way you are putting that, you have found from your own experience that when the story takes over . . .

PT: Yes, that's right. That's right. I have a strong feeling that you should never try to make a story go. I very seldom end by writing the story I set out to write, but I think it's because I'm interested in discovering what I think about something. I often don't know what I think about something, and so I begin writing a story. Here's an example I've given in other interviews. When I began writing, I was by no means a flaming liberal about Negroes, but I knew lots of stories about white people and Negroes, and I began writing them. I began to see who was getting the short end of it. With women too—I was not a great women's sympathizer, but I began writing stories about women and began to see who was getting the short end of the stick there.

JCR: So your writing was at least in part an education?

PT: Oh absolutely. That's to me what writing is. The truth is I don't like to think of myself as a professional writer. I think I write because I have to write out of a compulsion and not because I have to turn out a book every year. I write because I get great pleasure—great pain too, though. But then I write to discover what I mean and out of necessity. It's more like a religious experience than like a professional experience of a lawyer or doctor or something—it's not at all that way for me. It's something that I have to do, and I like it to be that way. In fact, Delmore Schwartz said to me about Caroline Gordon once, "Caroline's not a very good writer, but she's a real professional." That's death to me. I'd much rather he say of me, "He's on and off and not very well disciplined, but in this story, he's inspired." I think if you're inspired by things coming together, interpreting some part of life, I think that's [what's important].

JCR: You said some years ago that the best criticism of literature is literature itself, rather than critical commentary. How does some of the more aggressive modern criticism strike you? The work of the structuralists and deconstructionists?

PT: Oh, it just leaves me cold. I laugh about it, I'm sorry. Probably I'm stupid, but I just don't . . . I've talked a lot with E. D. Hirsch, who's involved in all that. I don't think they make sense. I think they're antiart, antiliterature. I don't think it's a benign thing going on.

JCR: When we talked earlier, you mentioned the influence that Tolstoy has had on you. In his writing it seems that he began with an overwhelming moral purpose and got carried away and wrote good stories anyway.

PT: I know. In spite of himself. But I think you do have to have that concern that he had, but I think that all the thoughts in the world and all the intelligence is no good without style, without knowing the right way to write it. They are absolutely equal, and the reason that art and literature offend some people is that the artist's style is just as important as the moral, and either is worthless without the other. There's no getting around that, I think.

JCR: Considering the rather cynical, clipped style of the typical *New Yorker* story, why have so many of your stories been in it?

PT: I never did quite know. I was so amazed from the very beginning. You know, I've hardly ever been in the *New Yorker* office. I don't even know the people. I often thought that they didn't know what my stories were about when they printed them, and they turned down any number of my best stories. It's hard to know why they did. Well, there are different people there; one hegemony will come in and then another. I don't know, unless they just read them as local color stories.

JCR: Tell me about the influence of your mother as a storyteller. You've said that the challenge in the feminine point of view was to take a different slant—a limiting factor to add a degree of difficulty and limitation to the story.

PT: Well I guess I was partly trying to find out why Mother told those stories. Everybody loved her stories, and she was full of witty things. This thing that happened in "The Spinster's Tale" really happened, about a drunk man coming by the house and all that, and her mother died when she was a little girl. But I made [the character] into a spinster because we used to say that Mother was like an old maid because she was such a puritan. Her brothers and sisters were not that way, but she was. And so I tried to interpret the story in her language. She would say funny things always. Lowell uses one of them in a poem, and I began to put it in my story and he said, "You can't do that. I've already used it." And I said, "I know, but it's my mother who said it."

JCR: Speaking of Lowell, you lead me to something else. Why were people as different—or as apparently different—from you as Lowell and Jarrell such close friends of yours?

PT: That was just "the not-me in thee I like." Lowell and I were so completely different, but we both were wild to write. Lowell and I were much closer than either of us was with Jarrell, really. It is hard to understand, but he [Lowell] was a driving, hard-working writer from the beginning, a classicist and all that. And I was always much dreamier and more intuitive, just writing and not thinking in terms of . . . and he always thought of himself in history as a writer. I always said we became good friends because we liked each other's jokes, and we got along that way and enjoyed people in the same way. We used to make great fun of Jarrell. We admired him tremendously. He was a little older—he was a teacher, you know; we were students. I got along with people a lot better than he [Lowell] did. Lowell was very difficult as a boy. He got to be different later. I was much more chasing girls and going out on the town, and yet I was serious too. That was part of it too; he was much more withdrawn and introspective.

JCR: There seems to have been in Lowell, as in so many other writers, a self-destructive urge, causing them to tear down their health or damage themselves psychologically from compulsions I don't suppose they can control. You seem so different from that. Is that stability largely a result of family as far as you are concerned?

PT: I don't know, I think it's a result of temperament, inherited probably. Lowell's upbringing was very difficult for him. He was the only child of very socially ambitious people, and proud, and critical. As I said earlier, my family was much more permissive and loving, and so those influences made us different. It was the attraction of opposites. I liked to go out, and he sort of liked to do it, and on the other hand, I liked the idea of working hard and studying and becoming a writer, and he was doing that.

JCR: We've talked about moral purpose and Tolstoy and related matters. How does Trollope figure into all this for you? I ask that because Mr. Warren said that he was glad that you could read Trollope because he couldn't, something like that.

PT: Well, I'll say in defense of Trollope's seriousness that he was admired greatly by Tolstoy and by Henry James. But the interest is to me in the individuals being developed at the same time as the context, the society they live in, and that's the very stuff of fiction, the interplay of the characters with the context of their lives. That's what Trollope, it seems to me, is all about.

I'll tell you, during the war I was stationed down in Somerset for a time, and I met an Englishman at a dance they had given there for the soldiers. And we got to talking—Mr. Abbott—and he lived in a great house nearby. We got to talking about literary things somehow, and he was wild about Trollope, you see, and I was there in Trollope country, near Salisbury and all. He urged me and gave me [books by Trollope] . . . and I was there camped out on the moors, and I could get these wonderful books. I began reading them then. It was terribly interesting to me to read Hardy and Trollope. Warren is wild about Hardy but not Trollope. I think the situations in Trollope are very profound, the relations, and I see a great influence on James. There are situations in James that are just taken right out of Trollope. I think there's a lot to be learned from Trollope in making us understand a character in terms of his environment, so that you really understand the English (upper classes at least) better through reading Trollope. I think that was the great thing for the novel—[showing] the class system, cast in a certain mold and then varying from it, as a character will.

JCR: You now seem to have gone entirely to writing novels. Is that right?

PT: I don't know. For the moment. I had begun this novel before I had a stroke last year, and it was a godsend to have something begun that I could work on just a little bit at a time. It saved my life in a way. I'm going to finish this novel, and I'm going to write another one.

JCR: Is this still entitled *To the Lost State?*

PT: Yes, and I think I'll stick to it. It's all about the "lost state of Tennessee," the lost state of Franklin. Before Tennessee was a state, they formed a state and called it the state of Franklin and tried to get admission to the Union. But North Carolina prevented it, and they went to war with North Carolina, and there was a pitched battle. So I was brought up in that tradition. My family were there, came in 1769 to East Tennessee. John Sevier was in that and all the early men of the state. They were finally defeated, and the state of Franklin was no more, and it was always spoken of as the "lost state of Franklin." The reason I'm using it is that I'm writing about the dissolution of the family in this, quite frankly. My grandfather was a senator, and he died in the Senate and was brought home on a special train to Tennessee. The whole novel takes place on this train ride, and all the hangers on, political and otherwise, were on that train. It took a week and it jumped the track, and I've heard about it all my life. The body was being brought home to Nashville for a state funeral, and he was finally brought here and buried in Knoxville and then was later moved to the homeplace. In the course of telling it and describing all the events and the characters that I think I know pretty well, I go back and talk for hours (for pages) about the past of all these people that are on the train, and then also I go forward and talk about what happens to them later.

JCR: There are a couple of things I would like to ask you about the South and Southern literature. I imagine you saw years ago what Walter Sullivan at Vanderbilt wrote—that the Southern Renaissance per se was dead. The implication of the article was that Southern literature as a discrete body of literature, as something identifiably unique, no longer existed.

PT: Well, some people have said in the last few years that the novel is dead. Usually the person who said it is somebody who feels he can't write it anymore; therefore, he feels that nobody can write. I don't think that's true. I think that there are certainly a lot of good Southern writers now, young ones. They don't have the cohesive element and the statement of philosophy or anything like that.

JCR: As I understood Sullivan's statement, it was not that there were not good Southern writers, but that Southern writers as a distinct body didn't have a very identifiable nature anymore.

PT: The thing is, the best writing in the South, say the Agrarians, it was simply a figure of speech. It was a mechanism, a way of saying something. They didn't believe literally—Allen Tate didn't believe— that the South would rise again, and I don't think John Crowe Ransom did. In fact, I've read Tate saying that every civilization needs a golden age to look back to. I think one of the best Southern writers now is James McPherson, the black writer, and I don't agree with a lot he says, but some of his fiction is just wonderful. It is inconceivable now to think of the South as being a separate culture. It's being completely invaded by other elements. How many people in Tennessee are living here now that have lived here for generations? It's entirely different.

JCR: Do you have mixed feelings there?

PT: Oh yes. Certainly. I hate the changing that way. There are moments when I am perfectly irrational about it and say they ought to . . . but there's no use in saying it.

JCR: In a 1970 essay Jan Pinkerton pointed out that you have have committed a "heresy" in Southern literature; instead of praising those who hopelessly hold onto the good things of the past, you tend to criticize these characters. The people who can't adapt get the roughest treatment in your stories. According to her convincing interpretation, you are saying that we must accept change.

PT: For me it's the debate that's interesting. I believe it's Isaac Singer that says you really don't think you know the answers to questions, but fiction is exploration. I'm not going to try to give the word that we must do this or that. I don't believe in politics, really, and I don't believe that we can cure the ills of the world through politics. It was much more possible to take the view that the Agrarians took in 1930 than it is now, and I regret it. The reason the South interests me primarily is that I think of it in terms of the family. I think this is the great loss to civilization, the death of the family. That's what I see occurring in this country [the loss of the family is what] we are threatened with, and maybe the whole world [is]. The South was the place where the family still operated more than any other place in the country.

JCR: You mention Singer. There seems to be a parallel there between cultural resistance and family survival and literary production with Jewish writers and Southern writers.

PT: Yes, I think so. There's much in common there. And Singer as a person reminds me of nobody so much as John Crowe Ransom.

JCR: Really?

PT: Oh, he's the gentlest, most courteous human being you could imagine. I don't know him well, but I've been with him a time or two.

JCR: You have mentioned that you work on several stories or several parts of a novel at one time and jump from one to another in a random fashion, as the mood strikes you.

PT: I'm not consistent from day to day in what interests me, and if I have several things going, I'll be much more inclined to work on one for a while. I don't think it's very profound, but you get dead on things sometimes. I do if I work on them day after day; yet I like to write all the time. I have several stories right now that I'll turn to. And this novel, I have now different parts of it going so that I can write on them.

JCR: So you still have some stories in progress?

PT: Yes.

JCR: I gather, then, that if something is not going well, you don't try to write through the bad spot and get to a good spot?

PT: No, I don't. I think they call that forced writing. It's always killing for me to force something through. If I'm not getting a great kick out of it, enjoying it, I don't want to write it. And I have written some bad stories. I've written stories in the *Sewanee Review* and others that I've never put in books. I wrote them with a theory. I didn't really have anything to write, and I got heavily symbolic—things that I don't really have much sympathy with. And I would sort of see how far I could go. I have a story in the *New Yorker* that I've never reprinted anywhere, "Uncles." The reason I've never reprinted it is that I had one of those contracts with the *New Yorker:* if you do four or six things within a year you get retroactively twenty-five percent of all you have gotten before. They wrote me and said, You have had so many stories within the last year, and if you get one more within the next three weeks, you get a bonus. And so I locked myself in my office, and I wrote the story, and they took it. And I've always been unwilling to print it. Really, it was the end of something. That was the answer to what we talked about. I knew what the *New Yorker* wanted in a story, and I gave it to 'em. [He laughs.] I was rather proud at the time to be able to do it, but then I felt a deep guilt. I didn't want to write that way, and I didn't write for them for some time. I felt sort of bewildered. Here I was mimicking myself.

[All of the bad stories] seemed like a theorem you worked out, and the story never took over and had a life of its own. . . .

I really like *In the Miro District*. I think maybe that's my best book.

JCR: Let me ask you about the final confrontation of Grandfather Manley and the boy. Why does the grandfather get so upset at the third confrontation, give up, and play the role everybody but his grandson wants? Is it just that he can't stand the idea of the boy's having a sexual relationship with a socially accepted girl? Has the boy crossed the last line of decorum?

PT: I think it's beyond hope now. That's my notion: that this ideal of a love that he would have in a society based on family just does not exist anymore. So he does everything that is superficial instead of trying to work at things, or work things out.

JCR: You use a refrain to the effect of, "If he had just struck me." When the grandfather finds him in bed with the "Eighth Avenue girl" and strikes him with the cane to wake him, the relationship between man and boy improves. This second confrontation shows progress in their understanding; but when the third one comes, with the nice girl naked in the chifforobe, the grandfather retreats entirely. He won't more or less fight it out.

PT: In the other he was still in there battling for him, but after this, it indicates that the [grandson] no longer has any of the values he has. That's my notion of it. I thought an awful lot about it at the time and tried to work it out. See, the parents have been very conventional people, and they wanted him to be the peacock on the lawn and all that. So he had put all his confidence in the boy. Then he saw that was useless, that the world he had tried to be realistic about had lost its values.

You know, one of my grandfathers (the other one, not the senator) was kidnapped like that, and my father went to get him.

JCR: Things left unsaid—the painful truths or the challenges or the criticism that would cause open friction—are important in your stories, as they are in the well-bred South, based on the idea that decent people don't say certain things. Here with Grandfather Manley, we are at the verge of a breakthrough, but it didn't quite happen. Or maybe it did, and then he withdrew. These silent conflicts are central in many of your stories, as in *A Summons to Memphis* and "Cookie" in particular. In what you have seen, does keeping these conflicts quiet in the South traditionally do more harm or good?

PT: I say, as I must about everything, to me it's the debate over whether they do or not. I don't know the answer to anything, in a way, and yet I'm eternally interested in asking these questions. You create stories weighting it one way so that this will seem to be true, and then another time, the other. To me this is what life is more like than working out a big system. You are constantly trying to ask the questions: Do families do more harm than good? Should Lee have gone to the mountains and the South . . . won the Civil War? There are parts of me that feel both ways, and that's why I couldn't be a lawyer. And the reason I can't write criticism, and wouldn't. The last piece of criticism I wrote was a review of Allen Tate's *The Fathers*. As soon as I can prove one thing in a piece of criticism (I knew it would be that way in the courtroom too) I can begin to think, "Well, on the other hand . . ." Being a lawyer, you can't do that way, and you can't as a critic, unless you got to be very sophisticated. My notion is [to write] fiction, and I'm interested in all these subjects of the South and the family. But I don't want to preclude any answer that might come. I don't know.

Just as I always felt: Some day I'll get religious. Some day I'll believe that religion was revealed by Jesus Christ and that we are going to be saved if we believe. Well, I've gone pretty far along, and I've almost become religious many times. I did. I became High Church Episcopalian for a time. And when Lowell became a Roman Catholic, I came very near. But I can't. A Christian will tell you, you have to have faith, but what is faith but turning your back on the other side, what you don't want to believe?

JCR: Is it not an embracing of mystery too, though? You accept mystery so readily in so much of what you write. The religious embrace seems to me more similar than different.

PT: Yes, I think so.

JCR: At least to me, an essential part of Christianity is the belief that we can only grasp so much. So much goes beyond what we can express, and that's okay.

PT: But I say, as I say about everything: And yet . . . and yet . . . That's the way I feel about nearly everything. To me this is not depressing because it's the very essence of life, wanting to know, not accepting anything absolutely, but always wanting to have your mind open. You say: Well, you go crazy doing that. But, on the other hand, you don't. You go on thinking and thinking about it. It's the way I think Chekhov must have felt a good deal about things, about religion and about politics too. I just admire his way. There are no heroes and no villains in Chekhov.

JCR: You mention Chekhov, but Tolstoy was very much the mystic, very much committed.

PT: Oh yes. And I admire that.

JCR: Do you think that hurt his art?

PT: No, I don't. I think it helped his art. I think we ought to be able to admire different kinds of writers because I can admire Tolstoy and Proust equally. And there couldn't be a more different view of the world. To me that's what's marvelous about it, to be able to like Flaubert and to like Joyce. For instance, the weak point for me in D. H. Lawrence [is what makes] his novels repetitious and tiresome, but he has got about a dozen stories that I just think are superb. I think "The Blind Man" and "The Horse-Dealer's Daughter" are wonderful. It's when he begins to get finite that it's not convincing to me anymore. When his stories get bad, it seems to me, is when he begins to really embrace doctrine. When he begins doing that, it's all over. But he has a body of stories that are among the greatest ever written. It's when people begin to stop inquiring [that their writing fails].

Part 3

THE CRITICS

Introduction

Even though reviewers have been almost unanimously complimentary, few critics have gone beneath the smooth surface of Peter Taylor's work. The selections that follow are excerpts from particularly helpful essays.

Robert Penn Warren was the first to label Taylor's milieu: the "urban middle-class world of the upper South." For years Taylor was the sole proprietor of this territory in short fiction. To his credit, he has exercised what Morgan Blum calls "self-limitation." His subtlety has been sufficient to cause some readers, like William Peden, to find a strong feeling of "austerity" in his stories, while others have discovered a gentle humor.

Despite disagreements as to whether his outlook is more negative or positive, recent critics have concurred with Jan Pinkerton on Taylor's surprising suspicion of the past. Herschel Gower points out a more readily apparent achievement: his skillful use of diction to portray well-bred Nashvillians between the world wars. Jane Barnes Casey emphasizes Taylor's faith in the new order, as well as his midcareer shift from female to male viewpoint characters. Finally, in his concluding marks from *Peter Taylor*, Albert J. Griffith focuses on the richness of character, conflict, and theme accomplished in the body of his work.

[Excerpts from the Introduction to
A Long Fourth and Other Stories]
*Robert Penn Warren**

Peter Taylor's stories are officially about the contemporary, urban, middle-class world of the upper South, and he is the only writer who has taken this as his province. This world which he delineates so precisely provides a special set of tensions and complications. For instance, the old-fashioned structure of family life still persists, disintegrating slowly under the pressures of modernity. . . . Lost simplicities and loyalties, the role of woman, the place of the Negro—these are topics which properly appear in the drama of this urban world. It is a world vastly uncertain of itself and the ground of its values, caught in a tangle of modern commercialism and traditions and conventions gone to seed, confused among pieties and pretensions. . . .

. . . If Peter Taylor is concerned with the attrition of old loyalties, the breakdown of old patterns, and the collapse of old values, he regards the process without too much distress to his personal piety. . . . The new world invites satire, and there is often a satiric component in Peter Taylor's treatment of it. In the whole effect, however, he stops somewhere short of satire. Rather, he presents an irony blended of comedy and sympathetic understanding. Uncle Jake of "The Scoutmaster" and Harriet of "A Long Fourth" are comic creations, but comedy does not exhaust them. We find an awareness of character beyond what explicitly appears. Peter Taylor has a disenchanted mind, but a mind that nevertheless understands and values enchantment. . . .

The skeptical, ironic cast of mind prompts a peculiar respect for the material it treats. Such a mind hesitates to impose itself on the material and to organize a story like a theorem. It can be satisfied only with a deeper strategy than is common, a strategy that will lure the reader on to his confusion. The reader who can accept the challenge of such a writer may pass through confusion to revelation. He will have reached the revelation, however, with a fuller sense of the complexities of things and of the shadowy, unsaid, unreconciled meanings that must haunt every story worth writing or reading. For such a writer, or reader,

*From the introduction to *A Long Fourth and Other Stories* by Peter Taylor, viii–x; copyright 1948 by Harcourt Brace Jovanich, Inc. Reprinted by permission of the publisher.

fiction is experience, not a footnote. And Peter Taylor's stories are not footnotes. . . .

. . . The style is secreted from the inwardness of the material and is an extension of the material. It has no substance of its own and offers nothing to come between us and the story. . . .

The stories of *A Long Fourth* are by a very young man. To recur to this fact is not to apologize for the performance here. Instead, it is to congratulate ourselves that we can look forward to many more stories from Peter Taylor. In the fullness of time he will write many more stories, stories probably deeper, fuller, richer, and wiser than these. But it is not probable that those unwritten stories will be any truer than these. I have said that Peter Taylor has a disenchanted mind. In terms of his very disenchantment, however, he has succumbed to the last and most fatal enchantment: the enchantment of veracity. And that is what, in the end, makes the artist free.

Peter Taylor: Self-Limitation in Fiction
*Morgan Blum**

Mr. Taylor has, from the beginning of his career, been able to imagine with such great verisimilitude people very different from himself in every way (in age, sex, race, fortune, and regional origin, for example) that few of the usual pathways to growth were available to him. As a writer, he matured young. . . .

In another sense, however, Mr. Taylor has limited himself to the autobiographical. Mr. Taylor's world is always a world he has observed, peopled with folk he has observed. He never writes of times he has never known, as the historical novelist does. . . .

I believe that certain other matters excluded from Mr. Taylor's fiction up to now can be explained partially, but only partially, on this same basis, that they lie more or less outside of his experience. One such exclusion is that of violence; Mr. Robert Penn Warren had observed its exclusion in Mr. Taylor's early stories, and it seems even

*This essay was first published by the University of the South in the *Sewanee Review* 70, no. 4 (Autumn 1962):559–78. Copyright 1962 by the University of the South. Reprinted with the permission of the editor.

more completely excluded in the stories written since then. Or rather, to put the matter more precisely, such violence as there is takes place off stage. We may see its results in character or even in the debris strewn about a wrecked office, but we never see it as action. . . .

Just as he avoids extremes in action, Mr. Taylor avoids extremes in characterization. He allows himself no male angels, no Alyosha Karamazov, and only a few female angels, who operate always in the restricted sphere of their own families. . . . This spreading of guilt—I shall come back to this in a later connection—characterizes Mr. Taylor's attempts to see people in their histories, with understanding and a measure of forgiveness. . . .

Mr. Taylor generally aims at a prose that resembles his villains in its lack of intensity. But it is a subtle instrument capable of rendering states of mind and feeling with great precision, of suggesting a character's point of view and even the "tone of voice" of his thought without ever being confined by this tone or the character's horizons. . . .

. . . Mr. Taylor's tremendous ability to give meaningful order to the parts of his stories plays a major part in the fiction's success. We are given everything we need to help us see why a character makes the key discovery that he does, but it is given with just enough indirection that we don't make our own discovery ahead of his. We might put the matter another way: Mr. Taylor's endings seem inevitable, but hardly predictable. . . .

. . . If he does not give us magnificent action scenes, he is one of the few writers to approach Tolstoy's talents in two other significant respects: (1) the ability to see in every act a man or woman performs some expression of that being's total history; (2) the ability to create real families and extremely moving scenes of family life. More than this, Mr. Taylor has achieved a third thing that we have no right to expect of a work as wide-ranging and inclusive as *War and Peace:* he has produced short stories that are perspicuous and unified gems.

William Peden

A Hard and Admirable Toughness: The Stories of Peter Taylor

*William Peden**

Contrasted to the technical experimentation of such a contemporary short story writer as Donald Barthelme or the unzipped frankness of a Robert Coover or the late Richard Farina, Peter Taylor's quiet and meticulously crafted fiction seems almost removed from contemporary reality, almost Edwardian. . . .

For it is time which is perhaps the most important force in Mr. Taylor's short stories, time and the past, a past which is like a ghost definitely uncomfortable in the clamour of post-Rooseveltian America. . . .

Consider Mr. Taylor's first collection, *A Long Fourth and Other Stories*, published in 1948. With the exception of a so-so "war" piece, all of these early stories are concerned with family relationships in respectable, urban, middle or upper middle class Tennessee. All of them depict the stresses and strains which are constantly undermining or threatening to undermine these family relationships. . . .

. . . Such confrontations between past and present and their effects on family relations have continued to furnish subject and theme for most of Peter Taylor's best stories. . . .

Most of Mr. Taylor's characters are similarly unable to escape from or forget the past; at the same time, they are not able to live very comfortably in the present. If in comparison to the world of much recent American fiction Peter Taylor's world is a relatively tranquil one, it is nevertheless a singularly cheerless one. Though it would be an over-simplification to label him either an optimist or a pessimist, his vision is extremely austere, increasingly so, it seems to me as his career has developed and deepened. . . .

. . . There is little warmth in his work. Humor, obviously, is not Mr. Taylor's concern: his readers may smile from time to time, but they seldom find themselves laughing [at] . . . an almost Thackerayan mixture of affection and contempt, humour and austerity, pathos and irony. . . .

In a seldom-remembered comment in his famous essay on Hawthorne's *Twice-Told Tales,* Edgar Allan Poe stated that the short story

*From the *Hollins Critic* 7, no. 1 (February 1970): 1–9. Reprinted by permission.

153

was a literary form which placed demands upon the reader commensurate with those placed upon the author; it demanded of the reader an art "kindred" to that of its creator. . . . The drama of Peter Taylor's stories tends to be internal. It exists in and flows from the inner lives of his people, inner lives which are only occasionally revealed in terms of dramatic external events or incidents. Character, indeed, *is* the story. . . .

. . . Within his self-imposed boundaries—limitations or weaknesses, some readers will find them—Mr. Taylor works quietly, surely, and effectively. The success of his fiction is the triumph of moderation. . . . Writing in prose which is characterized by simplicity and purity, he goes to the heart of universal personal and group relationships: why do human individuals act as they do, how does one's past effect his present, what are the relationships between an individual's responsibilities to himself, to his family, to the peculiar segment of society in which he finds himself? Such situations Peter Taylor explores with insight and understanding; it is difficult to think of any writer since James who depicts the nuances of such relationships more successfully.

The talkative old gentleman of "There" is referred to by another character as telling stories in "what seemed a mixture of masculine frankness and almost feminine gossipiness." To a degree, but only to a degree, this might be applied to the method of some of Mr. Taylor's stories. . . . He possesses an almost neoclassical distaste for excess, for the sensational, for the vulgar. . . . But there exists at the center of his vision a hard and admirable toughness, what earlier I have fumblingly called austerity, which is as far removed from "gentleness" as can be imagined. . . . a world in which, potentially at any rate, human life was respected, a world in which order and decency and decorum and a sense of responsibility and the value of love were held in high esteem. A pretty good world after all.

Jan Pinkerton

The Non-Regionalism of Peter Taylor: An Essay-Review

*Jan Pinkerton**

Perhaps many of Taylor's stories, in fact, have been read in terms of stereotypes—and of consequent value judgments, both favorable and unfavorable—that a closer examination would demonstrate to be inaccurate. The current collection, although containing only about half the author's published stories, nevertheless provides an opportunity for discovering some of the special qualities that take him far beyond the generalizations usually offered to explain lesser-known Southern writers. Taylor draws upon a specific milieu, to be sure, but he frequently entertains ideas that contradict the dogmas popularly believed to be the point of all Southern literature. . . .

. . . The character who mourns the past is usually shown by the author, through a variety of narrative techniques, to be limited in perception, to be ignoring obvious truths of the past, to be fantasizing an ideal age that never existed. . . . Taylor, however, is the analyzer of this phenomenon, not its true believer; he views the nostalgic stances of his characters with often-critical detachment, although ultimately he bestows the sympathy he always gives his imperfect human beings.

"Southern" themes of class-consciousness and of nostalgia, then, can be quickly spotted in Taylor's work but must not necessarily be identified with the author's own views. . . . He is not the mourner of the decline of the family, that institution traditionally considered the stabilizer of a society. He often records the discontinuities of contemporary family life, but he does not imply that families of the past were superior or preferable; there were always conflicts and neuroses, he makes clear, and even a seemingly stable family façade has always been blighted by the basic and constant flaws in human nature.

Most of Taylor's stories, then, have a Southern setting; most include characters who express a nostalgia for older times; most take place within a disordered family situation. Yet, as we have indicated, the chief substance of the stories is not these more obvious characteristics. . . .

*"The Non-Regionalism of Peter Taylor" originally appeared in the *Georgia Review* 24, no. 4 (Winter 1970):432–40, © 1970 by the University of Georgia. Reprinted by permission of the *Georgia Review* and Jan Pinkerton.

So the narrator of "Dean of Men" worries about his role as a man, and the narrator of "A Spinster's Tale" worries about how she, as a woman, will deal with men. We can identify, then, a basic theme in Taylor: a concern with role-playing and with personal identity. . . .

The ultimate statement on role-playing is to be found in "Miss Leonora When Last Seen," the story of an eccentric small-town spinster given to taking automobile trips in which she assumes various identities: the "great lady" in the lace chocker, the farmer's wife in dungarees, or, finally, the Memphis lady in stylish clothes looking for antiques or country hams. It is easy to say, of course, that Miss Leonora has lost her own identity because there is no longer a place for her in modern life or in a family that has dispersed. Yet her "real" self has always been problematic; no one has ever known her well, and the narrator admits that it is "hard for any two people to agree on what she is really like". . . . When people are seen solely in terms of their role—when human interaction is reduced to merely a kind of protocol—the result is loneliness and isolation. Miss Leonora, herself an abstraction and seeing others as abstractions, has always denied, and been denied, the benefits of human intimacy. . . . Perhaps her new facelessness, then, is essentially no different from the old; perhaps her new fluidity is even preferable to the stagnation of her previous life. We will return to what seems to be Taylor's heretical espousal of transcience, of motion, even of uprootedness. . . .

Indeed the most grotesque of all the Taylor characters in this collection are also those most attached to an idealized past: the old Dorset brother and sister of "Venus, Cupid, Folly and Time." They, too, play roles ("We are all young, we all love one another") and, like Miss Leonora, they cast the young people of the town into collective roles. . . . Thus the old people are defeated by being totally lost in abstraction, an abstract sense of their own lives, an abstract sense of the lives around them.

. . . Taylor lays no blame on the times, on modernization, on industrialism, on a new commercial economy. In a number of stories he explains what did go wrong: it was the failure of these people either to initiate change or to respond to change. . . .

. . . If it is easy to speak of the breakdown of the stable Southern family and the loss of old virtues, Taylor clearly countermands such facile conclusions in this story. Instead of lamenting decaying families, he introduces the question, *Why* is this family decaying? . . .

What is the moral of these stories? It seems to be: keep moving, be open to new experiences. The alternative is to stagnate. Yet is this a "Southern" theme or a Yankee theme? It sounds like the essence of the putative American experience, the official American code of conduct. The Southerners Taylor writes about, in other words, are those who stagnated because they did not move on, who fell into worship of an unreal past because they did not keep themselves refreshed by new ideas. This is Taylor's message, his heresy. He is a Southern writer who distrusts the past, a conservative writer who believes in change; those who see him as a stereotyped regionalist are themselves blinded by their clichéd responses to setting and style.

The Nashville Stories

*Herschel Gower**

It is a matter of biological fact that Peter Taylor is descended from Taylors on both sides. His mother Katherine Taylor was a daughter of Governor Robert Taylor of Carter County, East Tennessee. His father Matthew Hillsman Taylor was a native of West Tennessee at the other end of the state. Peter was born in Trenton in 1917 and because of his father's business moved often from one section to another. Each area is rich in materials for fiction, but it is in Middle Tennessee that Peter Taylor has found a setting for many of his stories. It is Nashville, the capitol of the state, that is often his *locus operandi,* the hub of his characters' actions. Nashville is often the place psychologically central to his first-person narrators. It functions as their point of reference, the place of established, stable values, the concentration of cultural mores.[1]

One of Taylor's narrators contrasts the uplands of East Tennessee with Nashville:

> The world [of Nashville] isn't the hard-bitten, Monkey Trial world of East Tennessee that everybody knows about but a gentler world in Middle Tennessee . . . which was known fifty years ago as the Nashville Basin and which in still earlier times, to the first settlers— our ancestors—was known somewhat romantically perhaps, and

*From *Shenandoah* 28, no. 2 (Winter 1977): 37–47. Reprinted by permission.

> ironically, and incorrectly even, as the Miro District . . . so called in
> honor of Don Estevan Miro, last of the Spanish governors of Spanish
> Louisiana . . .[2]

The city of Memphis—new, raw, bustling, a Mississippi River port
and cotton town—is two hundred miles away. When Taylor was growing up he heard his mother characterizing the differences between
East, Middle, and West Tennessee. In a recent interview, he said:
"She was a great storyteller, with a delightful sense of humor. Her
observations on the mores of Memphis, for instance, with its fast-paced
commercialism and emphasis on 'progress,' in contrast with Nashville's
more conservative pace, always delighted me."[3]

The importance of place in Southern fiction has already been explored by any number of critics. It can be noted here that in Taylor's
formative years very real distinctions could still be made among the
major cities of the three grand divisions of Tennessee. Some of these
distinctions are now rapidly disappearing and one city tends to look
like another from the Interstate Loop or the Belt Road. But each was
once a recognizable entity with its own social "outlook," speech patterns, and political stance.

Who, then, are Taylor's people—characters—individuals—the blood
and flesh of the stories? It has frequently been noted that he writes
only about upper middle-class Southerners who are not involved in acts
of bloodshed, lust, or violence. Taylor's characters, therefore, put the
author in a class apart from most contemporary Southern authors. His
characters live in the city, function as a family unit in spite of a great
many urban tensions, and display good manners at home and in the
social circles to which they belong. To generalize further: Taylor's
characters make a conscious effort to keep the family intact, and one
way of doing so is ritual—family dinners, entertainment in the home,
a succession of visits from relatives. None of these rituals could be
carried out in a cramped apartment or condominium with no servants,
and certainly not with the falling away of good manners. As gentle folk,
they have their problems with a changing world and with each other,
but they are never discourteous in addressing another human being or
confronting the world.

What they possess and hold on to and practice is a set of formal
country manners reminiscent of Jane Austen and eighteenth century
England. It is as though the country house in Miss Austen's rural society had packed up and moved (servants and all) to the West End

section of Nashville and settled in Elliston Place or Acklen Park or the suburbs and gone right on with established rituals. As a class these people may appear an isolated group in the modern Southern city and seem foreigners to its main currents. The truth is that they have not lost their close connections with the country. They have not cut themselves off from their background. That means that they retain an interest in an outlying county and keep in touch with cousins, friends, and older family servants in a small town somewhere beyond the periphery of the Nashville Basin. In other words Taylor's urban dwellers still cling, however futilely, to agrarian and feudal concepts of land and place. The Episcopal Church is so much taken for granted that it is seldom mentioned. . . .

Now we can move to a recurring theme in Taylor's fiction. In the interview with Louise Davis, Taylor said:

> The conflict that dominates many of my stories grows out of the shift of the Southern population from country life to city life. The real change in the world is represented there. When the South rises in industry, there are new elements in family life and mores. . . .[4]

As Taylor tabulates them, the losses that families sustain in moving from one place to another or living from one age to another are painfully evident. Not only is the integrity of the family at stake, the "sacred" individuality of its incorrigible and "unreconstructed" members may be sacrificed. In his latest story, published in the *New Yorker* in February, we see the grandfather, Major Basil Manley, as a holdout against the urbanization of body and spirit. Whereas the Major's children had come to Nashville and now "saw everything in terms of Acklen Park," the grandfather insisted upon living apart from them and in a county that was only on the periphery of Middle Tennessee. This Major Manley, a veteran of the Civil War, insisted upon a life of his own "free of the rules and mores" of life in Nashville. The narrator (and grandson) explains:

> . . . he went on living in the drafty, unheated farmhouse that he and his father before him had been born in. . . . That is to say, his farm and the county it was in were considered somewhat beyond the pale, not being in the handsome blue-grass, limestone country where livestock farms—and particularly horse farms—made the landscape a joy to look upon and where people had always held themselves well

159

above other mortal Tennesseans. He preferred to go on living over there even after my father had bought our fine house in Acklen Park and set aside the room there for his exclusive occupancy.[5]

This story is concerned with the family's attempts to "tame" the grandfather, divest him of his old-fashioned ways and bring him into town. A second theme in this story is the terrifying differences—always understated by Taylor—that exists between grandfather and grandson. Without them there would be no story, and, except superfically, the differences are never reconciled.

One of the many contradictions between the two generations is the way they look at women. The grandson explains:

> In our part of the world we were brought up on tales of the myste-
> rious ways of Thomas Jefferson, whose mother and wife are scarcely
> mentioned in his writings, and Andrew Jackson and Sam Houston,
> whose reticence on the subject of women is beyond the comprehen-
> sion of most men nowadays. Did they have too much respect for
> women? Were they perhaps, for all their courage in other domains,
> afraid of women or afraid of their own compelling feelings toward
> women? I didn't think all of this, of course, as I faced Grandfather
> Manley there in the hall, but I believe I felt it. It seemed to me that
> his generation and my own were a thousand years apart.[6]

It is a mark of Peter Taylor's genius that an issue as embattled as the War Between the Sexes and one so often overplayed today can be expressed in queries as polite as these. It is part of his charm as a writer to deal with the great issues without agitation or violence. An emotion is sufficient unto the day and time thereof, especially when there is a ripple of humor somewhere beneath.

This brings me to the point of saying that Taylor is indeed very, very funny. As Robert Penn Warren pointed out thirty years ago in his introduction to *A Long Fourth and Other Stories:*

> If Peter Taylor is concerned with the attrition of old loyalties, the
> breakdown of old patterns, and the collapse of old values, he regards
> the process without too much distress to his personal piety. The
> world he is treating, with its mixture of confusion and pretension,
> would appeal readily to a satiric eye.[7]

Then Warren goes on to say that in spite of the humor invariably associated with satire, Taylor is not a satirist. "In the whole effect . . . he stops somewhere short of satire. Rather, he presents an irony blended of comedy and sympathetic understanding."

Part of the humor that arrests us—and I suspect stops and amuses readers of the *New Yorker*—is the texture of the language and the rambling, anecdotal quality of the paragraphs. A story is seldom told as a straightforward experience, but with asides and digressions.

One contribution to the texture is the diction, which is faintly old-fashioned if not (at times) outright archaic. Taylor's people use phrases reminiscent of those suggested by Nancy Mitford twenty years ago when she and Alan Ross set the lexicographers buzzing over usages that they cavalierly designated "U" and "Non-U." As arbiters of distinctions between upper (or "U") and lower class (or "non-U") usage, the Honorable Nancy and Professor Ross cited "looking glass"and "writing paper" as Upper; they designated "mirror" and "stationery" as Non-Upper. It should be "spectacles," not "glasses," they said, and compiled their long lists of the levels of British diction in the twentieth century.[8]

Taylor's people are also inclined to follow certain speech patterns. They will say "boarding school" instead of "prep school." Men have their "toddies" before dinner—not "cocktails." "It amounted to *truck* farming, though we did not even say the word," one narrator confides. The couples may have tête-à-têtes in a sun parlor but never in a Florida room. After dinner they play cards in the "sitting room," not the "living room." Their houses at Monteagle and Beersheba Springs are always cottages—never cabins—no matter how rustic or what the scale. They attend "coming-out parties" instead of "debut balls." They regularly say "fetch" for "bring." They "quarrel" but do not "fight." They report that "swearing" took place on certain occasions but they never repeat the exact words. Husbands and wives may refer to each other as Mr. or Mrs., especially with servants, and on formal occasions they may address each other directly by title. "Cousin" is the other title most frequently used in the stories, but Colonel, Major, Captain, and Governor follow in close order. Matters of money are never discussed in actual dollars and cents. The "very rich" are either "affluent" or "people of means." (Only the vulgar will tell you how much they spend on anything from a child's rattle to a mansion in Belle Meade.) No wife or husband will criticize the other to a third party or speak disparagingly of an offspring—no matter what the child may have done to warrant condemnation. . . .

Unlike some of the people John Updike, Philip Roth, and Walker Percy write about, Taylor's Nashvillians are human beings who elicit compassion from us but do not strike us with terror. There is always the chance, however, that given another twenty years they will be just as terrible as the others. Perhaps Taylor is saying, finally, that by another generation these people will have outlived their Nashville period and come to the end of their uneasy period of Grace. As is the usual way of artists, Taylor has recorded a fragile company just in the nick of time.

Notes

1. I have used *The Collected Stories of Peter Taylor,* New York: Farrar, Strauss and Giroux, 1969. An earlier version of this paper was read at a conference on "The Urban South," Charleston, S.C., March 26, 1977.

2. "In the Miro District," the *New Yorker,* February 7, 1977.

3. *The Nashville Tennessean* [20 February 1977], interview with Louise Davis.

4. Louise Davis, loc. cit.

5. "In the Miro District."

6. Ibid.

7. "Introduction," *The Long Fourth and Other Stories,* New York: Harcourt, Brace and Co., 1948.

8. Nancy Mitford, "The English Aristocracy," *Encounter,* V. (Sept. 1955), 5–12.

A View of Peter Taylor's Stories

*Jane Barnes Casey**

As an author, Peter Taylor is more often praised than understood. The respect his work inspires frequently seems taken in by appearances, by the fact that in a formal sense, his material *seems* fixed. His stories usually take place in Tennessee—in Memphis or Nashville or Chatham; the characters are drawn from the upper middle class or from the Negro servant class; people are seen in terms of the family, rarely

*From the *Virginia Quarterly Review* 54 (Spring 1978):213–30. Reprinted by permission.

as isolated individuals or divorced ones or even single ones; the stories occur before 1960, and some take place around the turn of the century, while others are governed by the events and history of the 19th century, particularly, of course, the Civil War.

Yet the limitations Mr. Taylor sets on his work barely contain the shifting, probing attitude he constantly turns on his material. He is a great craftsman, but of a foxy sort, intent on working as much complexity as possible into the world behind his simple surfaces. In his best stories, his masterpieces, every detail is present in all its vital controversy; every part hums with its own inner fullness, as well as in its relation to every other part. He is a master of contradiction, though we have only to mention this quality when Mr. Taylor's singlemindedness must be accounted for. His work has always been concerned with the conflict between affectionate, civil society and chaos. . . .

The purpose of this essay is to discuss the way Mr. Taylor's handling of his recurrent themes has changed and evolved toward his newest collection of stories, *In The Miro District*. . . .

In The Miro District is basically about men. In two of the stories, the central characters are young men involved in rites of passage. Until this collection, Mr. Taylor has written more from the female point of view, using it as a screen through which he has observed disorder. Almost without exception, disorder has been associated with men trampling the social restraints enforced or represented by women. . . .

In "A Long Fourth," Mr. Taylor wrote out of identification with the large-hearted goodness of Harriet and Sweetheart; they were emblems of a coherent social world in which the younger generation had gone astray. . . . *In The Miro District* seems specifically organized to recapitulate Mr. Taylor's career, while demonstrating step by step his move from narrowest possible vision to the broadest, most humane one.

. . . In an author who once treated the same society so sympathetically, it is hard not to feel that "The Captain's Son" is literally a regional critique. The villain—though Tolliver proclaims it and Lila's family deny it—is in everybody's breast. The villain is snobbery. . . .

Both Tolliver and his father-in-law want to preserve a way of life, but they are willing to do it at the expense of life itself: Tolliver, after all, is impotent. Not coincidentally, Tolliver will not or cannot find employment. His impotence and joblessness are reflections of each other, and the connection of the two is the most powerful expression so far in Mr. Taylor's work of male despair in the modern world. . . .

But when the girl spends the weekend with the young narrator in

"In the Miro District," the event is both romantic and natural. It involves not the slightest social embarrassment for either the girl or the boy; being in love is enough to justify sleeping together (their embarrassment is only over being caught). Mr. Taylor writes as simply and directly of their weekend as if there had never been anything in his work to suggest that such an occurrence was ever forbidden. It's as if the book's progress were towards a full airing of things as they really were, beginning with a cry from the heart on behalf of the male, moving through a recognition of masculine passion and then, necessarily to the admission that women are passionate too. If Southern chivalry has snapped, it's because in some way it was false or reduced to empty appearances. . . .

"In the Miro District" provides this in its profound and economic use of the narrator's relation to his grandfather's frequently repeated stories. These stories are the crux of Mr. Taylor's story. They are unvarnished tales of "the eternal chaos we live in," and the grandfather insists on telling them instead of the Civil War stories he is expected to tell. . . . He refuses to submit to the stylized, domesticated version of chaos entertained by Southern society in its endless retelling of the Civil War. . . .

. . . When he finds the respectable girl naked in his wardrobe, he leaves and is not seen again until he's put on the social costume his family has wanted him to adopt all along. . . .

Given the drift of the whole collection, the grandfather's resignation is probably meant as his acknowledgement that traditional moral authority, based on the Southern woman's honor, is dead in his grandson's generation. . . .

. . . When he sees his own code dismissed by his grandson, the old man assumes the entire world of spirit has collapsed.

. . . "In the Miro District" revolves around the same conflict, but the outcome is different: if one world has clearly passed away, another has come in its place. It has always been part of Mr. Taylor's complexity that he saw how the new order brought new possibilities. . . .

Mr. Taylor repeatedly raises moral dilemmas only to show they can't be solved because there are no black and white moral categories. . . .

But there has been no loss of hope or of fulfillment. The ease attending the young lovers in "In the Miro District" derives from the eternal nature of love. Where Mr. Taylor once seemed to fear chaos, he now seems to trust the order inherent in experience: an order that does not depend on social restraint for its existence.

The Achievement of Peter Taylor

Albert Griffith*

Whatever recognition Peter Taylor deserves, he merits on the basis of his achievement in the short-story medium. His one novella, *A Woman of Means*, is too slight to build a reputation on, and his three plays have not yet been put to the test of professional production. He is reportedly working on a novel trilogy and a group of plays which may someday put him in the literary limelight.[1] In the meantime, he must be judged primarily on his accomplishments in short fiction.

Even here, in his favorite form, Peter Taylor's achievement is not that of an innovator. Taylor has compared himself to Trollope, and his position in the history of the twentieth-century American short story is indeed analogous to that of Trollope in the history of the nineteenth-century English novel. "There are two kinds of taste in the appreciation of imaginative literature: the taste for emotions of surprise, and the taste for emotions of recognition," Henry James noted in his essay on Trollope. "It is the latter that Trollope gratifies, and he gratifies it the more that the medium of his own mind, through which we see what he shows us, gives a confident direction to our sympathy."[2] Peter Taylor gratifies this same taste for emotions of recognition, and he gratifies it through much the same method which James attributes to Trollope— through his "complete appreciation of the usual." Another way of putting it would be to say that Taylor takes the commonplace subject matter of a William Dean Howells and runs it through the rarefied mind of a Henry James.

In neither technique nor theme is Taylor likely to seem startling or disturbing. Only in a few early stories does he try such self-conscious experimental techniques as dramatic monologue ("A Walled Garden"), montage structure ("Sky Line"), present-tense narration ("Allegiance"), and gothic setting and grotesque characterization ("A Spinster's Tale"). The techniques of his later stories are, generally speaking, far less contrived than these. Nowhere does Taylor employ the morbid subject matter, the disjunctive structure and style, the abstruse symbolism, or the scatological diction characteristic of many of

*Reprinted by permission from *Peter Taylor*, by Albert Griffith, © 1970, Twayne Publishers, 159–61.

his more famous contemporaries. He is never brutal, coarse, shocking; but neither is he precious, coy, titillating. The voice that speaks in his stories is essentially the voice of a gentleman—cultured but not dilettantish, ironic but not cynical, urbane but not foppish, sensitive but not sentimental. In short, Taylor preserves what was best in the genteel tradition in American letters without any of the mawkishness and prudery often associated with it.

Taylor's themes, like his techniques, neither exploit nor affront popular taste. There is little that is daring, inconoclastic, revolutionary in what Peter Taylor has to say. To note this characteristic, however, is not to say that he is banal or platitudinous. Limiting himself artistically to a narrow range of experience, Taylor nevertheless probes deeply within this circumscribed area, preferring generally to make a refinement on an old idea than to propose a totally new one. "And he has always been content to use his material; he never argues about it," Walter Sullivan has observed.[3] His own philosophic position seems one of mild, gentlemanly skepticism. Like Chekhov, he is more inclined to try to state questions correctly than to attempt definitive answers. He has, as Warren long ago pointed out, "a disenchanted mind, but a mind that nevertheless understands and values enchantment."[4] Thus, Taylor neither builds up new castles in the air from his own fancies, nor tears down those built by others. He has the rare gift of being able to criticize and appreciate simultaneously, to mix nostalgia and irony in a compound which retains the piquancy of both.

Peter Taylor's greatest achievement is probably his ability to create, within the restrictive confines of a short story, characters with a richness and complexity rarely found even in novels. "We care what happens to people only in proportion as we know what people are," James argued;[5] and Peter Taylor provides the proof for the dictum. Uncle Jake, Josie Carlson, Harriet Wilson, Sylvia Harrison, Aunt Munsie, Helen Ruth Lovell, the Tolliver family, Henry Parker, Matt Donelson, Franny and Miles Miller—these are the glory of Peter Taylor's art. "In the final analysis," William Peden has aptly said, "Taylor's fiction is meaningful because his characters are meaningful."[6]

In an age when alienation seems man's inevitable lot, Peter Taylor offers a quiet hope and consolation. When we read his stories, we are gently reassured that man has not yet completely lost the capacity to know and, on occasion, to love.

Notes

1. As early as 1954 Taylor was reported working on a novel entitled "A Rope from Hell to Hang Her With," a love story set in Memphis during the depression. This work, still in progress, is now planned as a trilogy. *A Stand in the Mountains* is the first of the series of plays Taylor is working on.

2. Henry James, "Anthony Trollope," in *The Future of the Novel*, ed. Leon Edel (New York, 1956), 259–60.

3. Walter Sullivan, "The Continuing Renascence: Southern Fiction in the Fifties," in *South: Modern Southern Literature in Its Cultural Setting*, ed. Louis D. Rubin, Jr., and Robert D. Jacobs (Garden City, 1961), 376–91.

4. Robert Penn Warren, introduction to *A Long Fourth and Other Stories* (New York, 1948), ix.

5. James, 240.

6. William Peden, *The American Short Story* (Boston, 1964), 61–68.

Chronology

1917   Peter Hillsman Taylor born 8 January in Trenton, Tennessee, to Matthew Hillsman Taylor (1884–1965) and Katherine Taylor Taylor (1886–1969).

1924   Moves to Nashville; since leaving, has returned regularly to visit family and friends.

1926   Moves to St. Louis; attends private grammar and college preparatory schools.

1932   Moves to Memphis.

1935   Graduates from public high school; works his way to England on freighter during the summer.

1936   Spring: studies under Allen Tate at Southwestern at Memphis (now Rhodes College); fall: attends Vanderbilt University; studies under John Crowe Ransom; meets Randall Jarrell and begins lifelong friendship.

1937   Leaves Vanderbilt and sells real estate in Memphis because Ransom now at Kenyon College and Taylor's father opposes his going there; publishes his first stories in *River* (a small journal in Mississippi): "The Party" and "The Lady Is Civilized." Randall Jarrell, as teacher, and Robert Lowell, as student, follow Ransom to Kenyon.

1938   Enters Kenyon in the fall; rooms with Lowell and begins another lifelong friendship.

1939   Ransom prints Taylor's only published poem in the *Kenyon Review*.

1940   Spring: graduates from Kenyon; fall: at Louisiana State University, begins graduate study in classes of Robert Penn Warren and Cleanth Brooks; drops out, preferring creative to scholarly work. Warren, editor of the *Southern Review* at LSU, publishes "A Spinster's Tale"; publication of this story and of "The Fancy Woman" (both written while Taylor at Kenyon) mark beginning of his mature work.

1941   Is drafted and writes letter requesting to be excused; woman who works at draft board and knows him assumes he is not serious and discards letter; is inducted into U.S. Army; spends war at Ft. Oglethorpe, Georgia, and at Camp Tidworth in England; is waiting in California to leave for Pacific Theater when Japanese surrender. (He says he was not a very good soldier, but he found his duties generally pleasant.) "The Fancy Woman" in Best American Short Stories (hereafter BASS).

1943   Marries Eleanor Ross on 4 June at Monteagle, Tennessee, in chapel of St. Andrews School.

1945   Publishes his first story in *Sewanee Review:* "Rain in the Heart," which is also in BASS; becomes instructor of English at the Woman's College of University of North Carolina in Greensboro.

1946   "The Scout Master" in BASS.

1948   Takes assistant professorship at Indiana University in Bloomington; publishes his first book, *A Long Fourth and Other Stories;* publishes his first story in the *New Yorker,* "Middle Age" (later collected as "Cookie"). Daughter Katherine Baird Taylor born 30 September.

1949   Returns to Woman's College in Greensboro, where Randall Jarrell is fellow teacher and next-door neighbor.

1950   Publishes *A Woman of Means;* awarded Guggenheim Fellowship for 1950–51; "A Wife of Nashville" in BASS.

1952   Receives grant from National Institute of Arts and Letters; goes to Kenyon as associate professor of English and drama.

1953   Appointed advisory editor of *Kenyon Review* (until 1958).

1954   Publishes *The Widows of Thornton.*

1955   Spends 1955–56 in Paris on Fulbright research grant; lectures at Oxford University. Son Peter Ross Taylor born 30 September.

1957   *Tennessee Day in St. Louis* first performed at Kenyon, and the play published.

1958   Spends summer and fall in Italy with the Jarrells and Robert Fitzgeralds.

1959   Publishes *Happy Families Are All Alike;* wins first prize in the O. Henry Award Stories (hereafter OH) for "Venus, Cupid, Folly, and Time," also in BASS.

1960 "Who was Jesse's Friend and Protector?" in BASS.

1961 Awarded Ford Foundation Fellowship to study drama in London; "Heads of Houses" in OH; "Miss Lenora When Last Seen" in BASS.

1963 Returns to University of North Carolina in Greensboro as professor of English; "At the Drugstore" in BASS.

1965 Awarded Rockefeller Foundation grant to write for a year. Randall Jarrell dies and Taylor is pallbearer at funeral. "There" in OH.

1967 Becomes professor of English at University of Virginia; edits with Robert Lowell and Robert Penn Warren, *Randall Jarrell 1914–1965*, a memorial book of reminiscences and critical essays.

1968 Publishes full-length play, *A Stand in the Mountains*, in *Kenyon Review*.

1969 Elected a member of National Institute of Arts and Letters; publishes *The Collected Stories of Peter Taylor;* "First Heat" in OH.

1970 "Daphne's Lover" in BASS.

1976 "The Hand of Emmagene" in BASS.

1977 Robert Lowell dies and Taylor is pallbearer at funeral. Publishes *In the Miro District and Other Stories*.

1978 "In the Miro District" in BASS.

1979 Awarded Gold Medal for Literature by the National Academy of Arts and Letters.

1980 "The Old Forest" in OH and BASS.

1982 "The Gift of the Prodigal" in OH.

1984 Retires from University of Virginia as emeritus professor of English; awarded Senior Fellowship by the National Endowment for the Arts.

1986 Awarded PEN/Faulkner Award for *The Old Forest and Other Stories*.

1987 Awarded Ritz Hemingway prize for fiction; awarded Pulitzer Prize for *A Summons to Memphis*.

Selected Bibliography

Primary Sources

(All primary sources are listed in chronological order.)

Collections of Stories

A Long Fourth and Other Stories. New York: Harcourt, 1948.

The Widows of Thornton. New York: Harcourt, 1954.

Happy Families Are All Alike: A Collection of Stories. New York: McDowell, Obolensky, 1959.

Miss Leonora When Last Seen and Fifteen Other Stories. New York: Obolensky, 1963.

The Collected Stories of Peter Taylor. New York: Farrar, Straus, and Giroux, 1969.

In the Miro District and Other Stories. New York: Knopf, 1977.

The Old Forest and Other Stories. New York: Dial Press, 1985.

Stories

"A Spinster's Tale." *Southern Review* 6 (Autumn 1940): 270–92. Collected in *A Long Fourth*, 1948; *Miss Leonora When Last Seen*, 1963; *Collected Stories*, 1969.

"Skyline." *Southern Review* 6 (Winter 1941): 489–507. Collected in *A Long Fourth*, 1948; *Miss Leonora When Last Seen*, 1963.

"The Fancy Woman." *Southern Review* 7 (Summer 1941): 65–92. Collected in *A Long Fourth*, 1948; *Miss Leonora When Last Seen*, 1963; *Collected Stories*, 1969.

"A Walled Garden," originally "Like the Sad Heart of Ruth." *New Republic*, 8 December 1941, 783–84. Collected in *Happy Families Are All Alike*, 1959; *The Old Forest*, 1985.

"Rain in the Heart." *Sewanee Review* 53 (Winter 1945): 23–43. Collected in *A Long Fourth*, 1948.

"The Scoutmaster," originally "The Scout Master." *Partisan Review* 12 (Summer 1945): 368–92. Collected in *A Long Fourth*, 1948; *The Old Forest*, 1985.

"A Long Fourth." *Sewanee Review* 54 (Summer 1946): 396–438. Collected in *A Long Fourth*, 1948. *The Old Forest*, 1985.

"Allegiance." *Kenyon Review* 9 (Spring 1947): 188–200. Collected in *A Long Fourth*, 1948; *Miss Leonora When Last Seen*, 1963; *The Old Forest*, 1985.

"Cookie," originally "Middle Age." *New Yorker*, 6 November 1948, 29–32. Collected in *The Widows of Thornton*, 1954; *Miss Leonora When Last Seen*, 1963; *Collected Stories*, 1969.

"Porte-Cochere." *New Yorker*, 16 July 1949, 21–24. Collected in *The Widows of Thornton*, 1954; *The Old Forest*, 1985.

"A Wife of Nashville." *New Yorker*, 3 December 1949, 42–61. Collected in *The Widows of Thornton*, 1954; *Miss Leonora When Last Seen*, 1963; *Collected Stories*, 1969.

"Their Losses." *New Yorker* 11 March 1950, 24–30. Collected in *The Widows of Thornton*, 1954; *Miss Leonora When Last Seen*, 1963; *Collected Stories*, 1969.

"What You Hear From 'Em?" *New Yorker*, 10 February 1951, 31–38. Collected in *The Widows of Thornton*, 1954; *Miss Leonora When Last Seen*, 1963; *Collected Stories*, 1969.

"Two Ladies in Retirement." *New Yorker*, 31 March 1951, 26–46. Collected in *The Widows of Thornton*, 1954; *The Old Forest*, 1985.

"Bad Dreams." *New Yorker*, 19 May 1951, 32–42. Collected in *The Widows of Thornton*, 1954; *Miss Leonora When Last Seen*, 1963; *The Old Forest*, 1985.

"The Dark Walk." *Harper's Bazaar*, March 1954, 120–214. Collected in *The Widows of Thornton*, 1954.

"1939," originally "A Sentimental Journey." *New Yorker*, 12 March 1955, 33–57. Collected in *Happy Families Are All Alike*, 1959; *Collected Stories*, 1969.

"The Other Times." *New Yorker*, 23 February 1957, 36–66. Collected in *Happy Families Are All Alike*, 1959; *Collected Stories*, 1969.

"Promise of Rain," originally "The Unforgivable." *New Yorker*, 25 January 1958, 32–51. Collected in *Happy Families Are All Alike*, 1959; *The Old Forest*, 1985.

"Venus, Cupid, Folly and Time." *Kenyon Review* 20 (Spring 1958): 169–202. Collected in *Happy Families Are All Alike*, 1959; *Collected Stories*, 1969.

"Je Suis Perdu," originally "A Pair of Bright Blue Eyes." *New Yorker*, 7 June 1958, 33–38. Collected in *Happy Families Are All Alike*, 1959; *Collected Stories*, 1969.

"The Little Cousins," originally "Cousins, Family Love, Family Life, All That." *New Yorker*, 25 April 1959, 38–44. Collected in *Happy Families Are All Alike*, 1959; *The Old Forest*, 1985.

"A Friend and Protector," originally "Who Was Jesse's Friend and Protector?" *Kenyon Review* 21 (Summer 1959): 395–418. Collected in *Happy Families Are All Alike*, 1959; *The Old Forest*, 1985.

"Heads of Houses." *New Yorker*, 12 September 1959, 52–87. Collected in *Happy Families Are All Alike*, 1959; *Collected Stories*, 1969.

"Guests." *New Yorker*, 3 October 1959, 48–89. Collected in *Happy Families Are All Alike*, 1959; *Collected Stories*, 1969.

Selected Bibliography

"Miss Leonora When Last Seen." *New Yorker*, 19 November 1960, 52–90. Collected in *Miss Leonora When Last Seen*, 1963; *Collected Stories*, 1969.

"Reservations: A Love Story." *New Yorker*, 25 February 1961, 37–72. Collected in *Miss Leonora When Last Seen*, 1963; *Collected Stories*, 1969.

"An Overwhelming Question." *Encounter* 18 (March 1962): 7–15. Collected in *Miss Leonora When Last Seen*, 1963.

"At the Drugstore." *Sewanee Review* 70 (Autumn 1962): 528–58. Collected in *Miss Leonora When Last Seen*, 1963; *Collected Stories*, 1969.

"A Strange Story," originally "Demons." *New Yorker*, 24 August 1963, 30–63. Collected in *Miss Leonora When Last Seen*, 1963.

"Two Pilgrims." *New Yorker*, 7 September 1963, 36–42. Collected in *Miss Leonora When Last Seen*, 1963; *Collected Stories*, 1969.

"There." *Kenyon Review* 26 (Winter, 1964): 144–70. Collected in *Collected Stories*, 1969.

"The Throughway." *Sewanee Review* 72 (Autumn 1964): 559–78. Collected in *In the Miro District*, 1977.

"Mrs. Billingsby's Wine." *New Yorker*, 14 October 1967, 56–60. Collected in *Collected Stories*, 1969.

"First Heat." *Shenandoah* 19 (Winter 1968): 28–36. Collected in *Collected Stories*, 1969.

"The Elect." *McCall's*, April 1968, 106–7, 168–69, 172. Collected in *Collected Stories*, 1969.

"Daphne's Lover." *Sewanee Review* 77 (Spring 1969): 225–50. Collected in *In the Miro District*, 1977.

"Dean of Men." *Virginia Quarterly Review* 45 (Spring 1969): 258–93. Collected in *Collected Stories*, 1969.

"The Instruction of a Mistress." *New Review* 1 (September 1974): 15–20. Collected in *In the Miro District*, 1977.

"The Hand of Emmagene." *Shenandoah* 26 (Winter 1975): 25–43. Collected in *In the Miro District*, 1977.

"Three Heroines." *Virginia Quarterly Review* 51 (Spring 1975): 269–81. Collected in *In the Miro District*, 1977.

"The Captain's Son." *New Yorker*, 12 January 1976, 30–50. Collected in *In the Miro District*, 1977.

"Her Need." *Shenandoah* 27 (Summer 1976): 3–8. Collected in *In the Miro District*, 1977.

"In the Miro District." *New Yorker*, 7 February 1977, 34–42. Collected in *In the Miro District*, 1977.

"The Old Forest." *New Yorker*, 14 May 1979, 34–48. Collected in *The Old Forest*, 1985.

"The Gift of the Prodigal." *New Yorker*, 1 June 1981, 42–52. Collected in *The Old Forest*, 1985.

Uncollected Stories

"The Party." *River* 1 (March 1937), 4–8.
"The Lady Is Civilized." *River* 1 (April 1937), 50–54.
"The School Girl." *American Prefaces* 7 (Spring 1942): 272–76.
"Attendant Evils." In *Vanderbilt Miscellany, 1919–1944*, edited by Richard Croom Beatty, 144–50. Nashville: Vanderbilt University Press, 1944.
"Uncles." *New Yorker,* 17 December 1949, 24–28.
"Nerves." *New Yorker,* 16 September 1961, 38–41.
"The End of Play." *Virginia Quarterly Review* 41 (Spring 1965): 248–65.
"A Cheerful Disposition." *Sewanee Review* 75 (Spring 1967): 243–65.
"Tom, Tell Him." *Sewanee Review* 76 (Spring 1968): 159–86.
"The Early Guest." *Shenandoah* 24 (Winter 1973): 21–43. Reprint. *The Early Guest (a sort of story, a sort of play, a sort of dream)*. Winston-Salem: Palaemon Press, 1982. This is a chapbook; 140 copies were printed, 100 for sale, each signed by the author and numbered.
"The Megalopolitans." *Ploughshares* 2, 4 (1975).

Novels

A Woman of Means. New York: Harcourt, 1950. Republished by Frederick C. Beil in 1984.
A Summons to Memphis. New York: Knopf, 1986.

Drama

"The Death of a Kinsman: A Play." *Sewanee Review* 57 (Winter 1949): 86–119. Collected in *The Widows of Thornton*, 1954; *Miss Leonora When Last Seen and Fifteen Other Stories*, 1963; *The Old Forest*, 1985.
Tennessee Day in St. Louis: A Comedy. New York: Random House, 1957. Act 1 originally published as "Tennessee Day in St. Louis." *Kenyon Review* 18 (Winter 1956): 92–119.
"A Stand in the Mountains." *Kenyon Review* 25 (March 1968): 169–264. Also published under hard cover by Frederick C. Beil in 1986.
Presences: Seven Dramatic Pieces. Boston: Houghton Mifflin, 1973.

Miscellaneous Works

"The Furnishings of a House." *Kenyon Review* 1 (Summer 1939): 308. Taylor's only published poem.
Lowell, Robert, Peter Taylor, and Robert Penn Warren, eds. *Randall Jarrell: 1914–1965*. New York: Farrar, Straus, and Giroux, 1967.

Secondary Sources

Bibliographies

Griffith, Albert J. *Peter Taylor*. Boston: Twayne, 1970. This volume is primarily devoted to critical commentary on the body of Taylor's work through 1969. It is also notable, however, for its good brief biography and its extremely thorough bibliography of primary and critical sources.

Kramer, Victor A., Patricia A. Bailey, Carol G. Dana, and Carl H. Griffin. *Andrew Lytle, Walker Percy, Peter Taylor: A Reference Guide*. Boston: G.K. Hall, 1983.

Interviews

Davis, Louise. "Who Was That Ward-Belmont Girl Nude in the Closet?" *Nashville Tennessean*, 20 February 1977, sec. E, 1.

Evory, Ann and Linda Metzger, eds. "Taylor, Peter (Hillsman)." In *Contemporary Authors*, New Revision Series, vol. 9, 487–91. Detroit: Gale, 1983. Contains an interview by Jean W. Ross.

Goodwin, Stephen. "An Interview with Peter Taylor." *Shenandoah* 24 (Winter 1973): 3–20.

Jordan, Jenice. "He 'Writes for Fun,' but His Stories Sell." *Columbus* [Ohio] *Dispatch*, 6 December 1959, 10.

La Badie, Donald. "Peter Taylor." [Memphis] *Commercial Appeal*, 5 October 1986, sec. J, 1–2.

Paine, J. H. E. "Interview with Peter Taylor." The interview was conducted 1 March 1986 and will appear in *Journal of the Short Story in English* 9 (Fall 1987): 14–35.

Sides, W. Hampton. "Peter Taylor." *Memphis*, February 1987, 109–17.

Criticism

Baumbach, Jonathan. *Modern and Contemporaries: Nine Masters of the Short Story*, 343–44. New York: Random House, 1968.

Blum, Morgan. "Peter Taylor: Self-Limitation." *Sewanee Review* 70 (1962): 559–78.

Brown, Ashley. "The Early Fiction of Peter Taylor." *Sewanee Review* 70 (1962): 588–602.

Broyard, Anatole. Review of *In the Miro District and Other Stories*. *New York Times Book Review*, 3 April 1977, 4.

Casey, Jane Barnes. "A View of Peter Taylor's Stories." *Virginia Quarterly Review* 54 (1978): 213–30.

Selected Bibliography

Cathy, Kenneth Clay. "Peter Taylor: An Evaluation." *Western Review* 18 (1953): 9–19.

Clemons, Walter. "Southern Comfort." *Newsweek*, 11 March 1985, 74.

Eder, Richard. Review of *The Old Forest and Other Stories. Los Angeles Times Book Review*, 3 February 1985, 1.

Eisinger, Chester E. *Fiction of the Forties*, 196–98. Chicago: University of Chicago Press, 1963.

Gass, William H. "Look at Me . . ." *New York Times Book Review*, 19 October 1969, 5, 44.

Goodwin, Stephen. "Life Studies." *Shenandoah* 21 (Winter 1970): 100–102.

Gower, Herschel. "The Nashville Stories." *Shenandoah* 28 (Winter 1977): 37–47.

Gray, Richard. *The Literature of Memory: Modern Writers of the American South.* Baltimore: Johns Hopkins University Press, 1977.

Griffith, Albert J. *Peter Taylor*. Boston: Twayne, 1970.

Gunton, Sharon R., ed. "Taylor, Peter." In *Contemporary Literary Criticism*, vol. 18, 522–29. Detroit: Gale, 1981.

Holman, David Marion. "Peter Taylor." In *The History of Southern Literature*, edited by Louis D. Rubin, Jr., et al., 494–96. Baton Rouge: Louisiana State University Press, 1985.

Howard, Richard. "Twenty-one Holding Actions by a Modest American Master." *New York Times Book Review*, 19 October 1969, 4, 26.

James, Caryn. "Symbols and Themes Mature into Plots." *New York Times Book Review*, 17 February 1985, 26.

Kazin, Alfred. *The Bright Book of Life: American Novelists and Storytellers from Hemingway to Mailer*, 46–49. Boston: Little, Brown, 1973.

Kerman, Michael. "Peter Taylor and the Layers of Life." *Washington Post*, 4 March 1985, sec. B, 1.

Kinsman, Clare D., ed. "Taylor, Peter (Hillsman)." In *Contemporary Authors*, vols. 13–16, 794–95. Detroit: Gale, 1975.

Leader, Zachary. "Old Times in the New South." [London] *Times Literary Supplement*, 22 January 1982, 4112, 75–76.

Lytle, Andrew. "The Displaced Family." *Sewanee Review* 66 (1958): 115–20.

McDowell, Edwin. 'For Storyteller, 69, New Recognition." *New York Times*, 7 May 1986, 25.

Marowski, Daniel G., ed. "Peter (Hillsman) Taylor." In *Contemporary Literary Criticism*, vol. 37, 406–14. Detroit: Gale, 1986.

Oates, Joyce Carol. "Realism of Distance, Realism of Immediacy." *Southern Review* 7 (Winter 1971): 295–313. Only pages 299–302 on Taylor.

Opdahl, Keith. "His Stories Lay Quiet Siege." *Christian Science Monitor*, 22 January 1970, 11.

Peden, William. *The American Short Story: Continuity and Change 1940–1975*, 2d ed. Boston: Houghton Mifflin, 1975.

———. "A Hard and Admirable Toughness." *Hollins Critic* 7 (February 1970): 1–9.

Pinkerton, Jan. "A Critical Distortion of Peter Taylor's 'At the Drugstore.'" *Notes on Contemporary Literature* 1, no. 4 (1971): 6–7.

———. "The Vagaries of Taste and Peter Taylor's 'A Spinster's Tale.'" *Kansas Quarterly* 9 no. 2 (1977): 81–85.

Raskin, Barbara. "Southern-Fried." *New Republic* 18 October 1969, 29–30.

Riley, Carolyn, ed. "Taylor, Peter." In *Contemporary Literary Criticism*, vol. 1, 333–35. Detroit: Gale, 1973.

———. "Taylor, Peter." In *Contemporary Literary Criticism*, vol. 4, 542–43. Detroit: Gale, 1975.

Robinson, Clayton. "Peter Taylor." In *Literature of Tennessee*, edited by Ray Willbanks, 149–61. Rome, Georgia: Mercer University Press, 1984.

Sale, Roger. "Its Discontent." *Hudson Review* 22 (Winter 1970): 710.

Sims, Barbara B. "Symbol and Theme in Peter Taylor's 'A Wife of Nashville.'" *Notes on Modern American Literature* 2 (1978): item 22.

Sullivan, Walter. "The Continuing Renaissance: Southern Fiction in the Fifties." In *South: Modern Southern Literature in Its Cultural Setting*, edited by Louis D. Rubin and Robert D. Jacobs, 389–91. Garden City, N.Y.: Doubleday, 1961.

———. "In Time of the Breaking of the Nations: The Decline of Southern Fiction." In *Death by Melancholy: Essays on Modern Southern Fiction*, 87–96. Baton Rouge: Louisiana State University Press, 1972.

Tate, Allen. "Peter Taylor." *Shenandoah* 20 (Winter 1977): 10.

Thompson, John. "The Clever, the True, and the Marvelous." *Harper's*, November 1969, 127–34.

Towers, Robert. "A Master of the Miniature Novel." *New York Times Book Review*, 17 February 1985, 1 and 26.

Williamson, Alan. "Identity and the Wider Eros: A Reading of Peter Taylor's Stories." *Shenandoah* 30 (Fall 1978): 71–84.

Yardley, Jonathan. "Peter Taylor: The Quiet Virtuoso." *Book World—Washington Post*, 27 January 1985, 3.

———. "Rewarding a Master Writer." *Washington Post*, 20 August 1984, sec. C, 1.

———. "Taylor's South." *New Republic*, 22 November 1969, 27–29.

Young, Thomas Daniel. "The Contemporary Scene." In *Tennessee Writers*, 77–111. Knoxville: University of Tennessee Press, 1981.

Index

Index

About the Author

James Curry Robison, born in 1947 in Lebanon, Tennessee, and graduated from Westminster School in Atlanta, read his first story by Peter Taylor ("A Spinster's Tale") when he was a freshman at Vanderbilt. Having lived outside the South as a child, gone to Vanderbilt, and published stories, he has these experiences in common with Taylor.

He earned his master's degree at Middle Tennessee and his doctorate at Oklahoma State. He has published stories in the *Vanderbilt Review, Cimarron Review, Chariton Review,* and *Texas Review.* His essays have appeared in *Chariton Review, Mid-American Review,* and *A Cyclopedia of Short Fiction.* Most recently he wrote the portion of Twayne's *The American Short Story: A Critical History* covering 1969 to 1980.

He is currently head of the English Department at Brentwood Academy, near Nashville, Tennessee.

About the Editor

General editor Gordon Weaver earned his B.A. in English at the University of Wisconsin-Milwaukee in 1961; his M.A. in English at the University of Illinois, where he studied as a Woodrow Wilson Fellow, in 1962; and his Ph.D. in English and creative writing at the University of Denver in 1970. He is the author of several novels, including *Count a Lonely Cadence, Give Him a Stone, Circling Byzantium,* and most recently *The Eight Corners of the World* (Vermont: Chelsea Green Publishing Company, 1988). Many of his numerous short stories are collected in *The Entombed Man of Thule, Such Waltzing Was Not Easy, Getting Serious, Morality Play,* and *A World Quite Round.* Recognition of his fiction includes the St. Lawrence Award for Fiction (1973), a National Endowment for the Arts Fellowship (1974), and the O. Henry First Prize (1979). He edited *The American Short Story, 1945–1980: A Critical History.* He is a professor of English at Oklahoma State University and serves as an adjunct member of the faculty of the Vermont College Master of Fine Arts in Writing Program. Married, and the father of three daughters, he lives in Stillwater, Oklahoma.